TOP 101
WOMEN OF STEM

EDITED BY NICHOLAS FAULKNER

Britannica®
Educational Publishing

IN ASSOCIATION WITH

ROSEN
EDUCATIONAL SERVICES

Published in 2017 by Britannica Educational Publishing (a trademark of Encyclopædia Britannica, Inc.) in association with The Rosen Publishing Group, Inc.
29 East 21st Street, New York, NY 10010

Distributed exclusively by Rosen Publishing.
To see additional Britannica Educational Publishing titles, go to rosenpublishing.com.

First Edition

Britannica Educational Publishing
J.E. Luebering: Director, Core Reference Group
Anthony L. Green: Editor, Compton's by Britannica

Rosen Publishing
Nicholas Faulkner: Editor
Nelson Sá: Art Director
Michael Moy: Designer
Cindy Reiman: Photography Manager
Karen Huang: Photo Researcher
Introduction and supplementary material by Dr. Nicki Peter Petrikowski

Library of Congress Cataloging-in-Publication Data

Names: Faulkner, Nicholas, editor.
Title: 101 women of STEM / edited by Nicholas Faulkner.
Other titles: One hundred one women of STEM
Description: First edition. | New York : Britannica Educational Publishing in
  association with Rosen Educational Services, 2017. | Š2017 | Series:
  People you should know
Identifiers: LCCN 2016001886 | ISBN 9781680485110 (library bound : alk. paper)
Subjects: LCSH: Women scientists--Biography--Juvenile literature. | Women in
  science--History--Juvenile literature. | Science--Biography--Juvenile literature. | Science-
  -History--Juvenile literature. | Women in technology--History--Juvenile literature. |
  Technology--Biography--Juvenile literature. | Technology--History--Juvenile literature.
Classification: LCC Q141 .A1584 2017 | DDC 509.2/2--dc23
LC record available at http://lccn.loc.gov/2016001886

Manufactured in China

CONTENTS

9

20

36

55

77

79

90

106

124

INTRODUCTION

The academic disciplines of science, technology, engineering, and mathematics are widely considered to be a male domain, and not without reason. Historically, men have outnumbered women in STEM fields by a vast margin, and while the gap has been getting smaller in recent years, it is still pronounced, with only about a quarter of the people working in science, technology, engineering, and mathematics in the United States being female. Despite political campaigns aiming to increase the number of women involved in STEM fields, relatively few choose to pursue a career in these areas, and as a result gender balance, which has been increased considerably in other formerly male-dominated fields of work like business and law, lags behind in science, technology, engineering, and mathematics.

The negative stereotype of girls being bad at math still persists, even though it has been proven wrong. Studies have shown that there is no biological reason for females being worse at math than males, but the existence of this deep-rooted bias itself can lead to insecurity and girls being discouraged from participating in activities that require mathematical skills. Due to the low number of women in STEM fields, a lack of female role models in girls' lives may also play a part. But even though you may not know them personally, there are a great number of women who have made significant contributions to STEM fields.

People You Should Know: 101 Women of STEM presents the biographies of female scientists, technologists, engineers, and mathematicians who have reduced the negative prejudice against women in their disciplines to absurdity by their example and who are an inspiration for everybody.

Despite the male domination of the field, women have made valuable contributions to science all throughout history. Hypatia of Alexandria was a renowned philosopher, mathematician, astronomer, and inventor in 4th century Egypt. Maria Sibylla Merian paved the way for entomology with her illustrations of insects made in the late 17th and early 18th centuries. And 19th-century mathematician Ada

King, countess of Lovelace, is regarded as the world's first computer programmer.

It took some time and effort, however, until women were accepted into the academic world. Elena Cornaro was the first woman to receive a doctoral degree from a university in 1678. Laura Bassi became the first female physics professor at a European university in 1732, followed by Maria Gaetana Agnesi, who was appointed as professor of mathematics in Bologna in 1750.

Florence Nightingale revolutionized health care by establishing high professional standards in nursing, and she taught at the medical school for women cofounded in 1874 by Elizabeth Garrett Anderson, who had been refused admission to medical schools but nonetheless went on to become the first female member of the British Medical Association. In the United States, the acceptance of women in the medical field was promoted by Emily Blackwell, and the contributions to medicine made by female physicians and medical scientists like Clelia Duel Mosher, Alice Hamilton, Florence Rena Sabin, Sara Josephine Baker, Helen Brooke Taussig, Virgina Apgar, and Rosalyn Sussman Yalow make clear that excluding women from the field for a long time was not a smart idea.

Astronomers such as Caroline Herschel, Maria Mitchell, Mary Watson Whitney, Williamina Paton Stevens Fleming, Annie Jump Cannon, Henrietta Swan Leavitt, Cecilia Payne-Gaposchkin, and Jocelyn Bell Burnell have furthered our understanding of how the universe works. And of course there have been female astronauts like Valentina Tereshkova and Helen Sharman who have crossed the final frontier.

Discouraging women from getting involved in science, technology, engineering, and mathematics for a long time has undoubtedly been to the detriment of humankind, and using all of the brain power available can only benefit us all.

ELIZABETH CABOT AGASSIZ

(b. 1822—d. 1907)

Elizabeth Cabot Agassiz née Elizabeth Cabot Cary was an American naturalist and educator who was the first president of Radcliffe College, Cambridge, Massachusetts.

Elizabeth Cary was related to many of Boston's leading families. She received no formal schooling but acquired a somewhat haphazard education at home. In April 1850 she married the distinguished and recently widowed Swiss naturalist Louis Agassiz; her work proved to be invaluable to his career. Her notes on his lectures were the raw material of much of his published work, and she helped organize and manage several of his expeditions into the field, notably the Thayer Expedition to Brazil in 1865-66 and the Hassler Expedition through the Strait of Magellan in 1871-72. Together they founded the coeducational Anderson School of Natural History, a marine laboratory on Penikese Island in Buzzard's Bay, Massachusetts. Elizabeth Agassiz's own published work includes *A First Lesson in Natural History* (1859), *Seaside Studies in Natural History* (1865; with her stepson Alexander Agassiz), and *A Journey in Brazil* (1867; with her husband).

From 1855 to 1863 in their Cambridge home, Elizabeth Agassiz conducted a school for girls, which, in addition to providing a needed supplement to the family income, was a pioneering effort in women's education. For some years after the death of her husband in 1873, she devoted herself to the care of her grandchildren and to the writing of a memoir of her husband. The book was published as *Louis Agassiz: His Life and Correspondence* (1885).

From the time of her husband's death Agassiz had been interested in the idea of a college for women to be taught by the Harvard University faculty; a coordinate college would give women access to educational resources once reserved for men. In 1879 she helped open the "Harvard Annex" in Cambridge and was named president when it was incorporated as the Society for the Collegiate Instruction of Women. In 1894 the college was named Radcliffe in honor of Ann Radcliffe, founder of the first Harvard scholarship (1643), and was formally linked to Harvard University. Agassiz remained president of the college until 1899, when she relinquished her formal duties.

MARIA GAETANA AGNESI

(b. 1718—d. 1799)

Maria Gaetana Agnesi was an Italian mathematician and philosopher, considered to be the first woman in the Western world to have achieved a reputation in mathematics.

Agnesi was the eldest child of a wealthy silk merchant who provided her with the best tutors available. She was an extremely precocious child who mastered Latin, Greek, Hebrew, and several modern languages at an early age, and her father liked to host gatherings where she could display her knowledge. *Propositiones philosophicae* ("Propositions of Philosophy"), a series of essays on natural philosophy and history based on her discussions before such gatherings, was published in 1738.

Agnesi's best-known work, *Instituzioni analitiche ad uso della gioventù italiana* (1748; "Analytical Institutions for the Use of Italian Youth"), in two huge volumes, provided a remarkably comprehensive and systematic treatment of algebra and analysis, including such relatively new developments as integral and differential calculus. In this text is found a discussion of the Agnesi curve, a cubic curve known in Italian as versiera, which was confused with versicra ("witch") and translated into English as the "Witch of Agnesi." The French Academy of Sciences, in its review of the *Instituzioni*, stated that: "We regard it as the most complete and best made treatise." Pope Benedict XIV was similarly impressed and appointed Agnesi professor of mathematics at the University of Bologna in 1750.

However, Agnesi had turned increasingly to religion and never journeyed to Bologna. After the death of her father in 1752, she devoted herself almost exclusively to charitable work and religious studies. She established various hospices and died in one of the poorhouses that she had once directed.

FRANCES E. ALLEN

(b. 1932)

Frances E. Allen is an American computer scientist and in 2006 was the first woman to win the A.M. Turing Award, the highest honour in computer science, for her "pioneering contributions to the theory and practice of optimizing compiler techniques that laid the foundation for modern optimizing compilers and automatic parallel execution."

Frances E. Allen

Allen received a bachelor's degree (1954) in mathematics from Albany State Teachers College (now the State University of New York, Albany) and a master's degree (1957) in mathematics from the University of Michigan. Shortly after graduation Allen joined IBM's Thomas J. Watson Research Center, where she was first hired to teach staff scientists a new computer programming language named FORTRAN. During the 1960s Allen worked on compilers for IBM supercomputers, such as the IBM 7030 (known as Stretch) and the IBM 7950 (known as Harvest), that were ordered by the U.S. National Security Agency for delivery to Los Alamos National Laboratory. Much of her subsequent work concerned efficient computer programming for multiprocessing systems, especially her work with the Parallel TRANslation Group (PTRAN), which she founded in the early 1980s. She was named an IBM fellow in 1989, the first woman so honoured, and president of the IBM Academy of Technology (1995). Allen retired in 2002.

Throughout most of her career, Allen held visiting lectureships at various universities. She also served on the U.S. National Science Foundation (1972—78). Allen was elected to the U.S. National Academy of Engineering (1987), the Institute of Electrical and Electronics Engineers, the Association for Computing Machinery, the American Academy of Arts and Sciences, and the American Philosophical Society (2001). In addition to the Turing Award, Allen received the 2002 Augusta Ada Lovelace Award from the Association of Women in Computing.

ELIZABETH GARRETT ANDERSON

(b. 1836—d. 1917)

Elizabeth Garrett Anderson was an English physician who advocated the admission of women to professional education, especially in medicine.

Refused admission to medical schools, Anderson began in 1860 to study privately with accredited physicians and in London hospitals and was licensed to practice in 1865 by the Society of Apothecaries. She was appointed (1866) general medical attendant to the Marylebone

Dispensary, later the New Hospital for Women, where she worked to create a medical school for women. In 1918 the hospital was renamed Elizabeth Garrett Anderson Hospital in her honour.

Anderson received the M.D. degree from the University of Paris in 1870, and in 1908 she became the first woman mayor of Aldeburgh.

MARY ANNING

(b. 1799—d. 1847)

A prolific English fossil hunter and amateur anatomist Mary Anning is credited with the discovery of several dinosaur specimens that assisted in the early development of paleontology. Her excavations also aided the careers of many British scientists by providing them with specimens to study and framed a significant part of Earth's geologic history. Some scientists note that fossils recovered by Anning may have also contributed, in part, to the theory of evolution put forth by English naturalist Charles Darwin.

Anning was born on May 21, 1799, in Lyme Regis, Dorset, England. She was one of two surviving children born to cabinetmaker and amateur fossil collector Richard Anning and his wife, Mary Moore. The family relied on the sale of fossils collected from seaside cliffs near their home along England's Channel coast as a source of income. After Richard's death in 1810, the family mainly relied on charity. Mary, her brother, Joseph, and their mother, who were skilled fossil collectors themselves, supplemented their meager resources by selling fossils of invertebrates, such as ammonoids and belemnoids, to collectors and scholars. In 1817 the fossils attracted the attention of British fossil collector Lieutenant Colonel Thomas Birch, who assisted the family financially by purchasing a number of specimens. Later he auctioned off his collection and donated the proceeds to the Anning family during a particularly desperate period in their lives.

Over the course of her life, Mary Anning also discovered the remains of several large vertebrates embedded in the cliffs of Lyme Regis. The cliffs, which date from the late Triassic to early Jurassic periods (some

229 million to 176 million years ago), a time when the area was submerged and located closer to the Equator, contain the fossil-rich limestone and shale of the Blue Lias formation. In 1810 her brother found the first known Ichthyosaurus specimen; however, she was the one who excavated it, and some sources also give her credit for the discovery. British physician Everard Home described the specimen shortly thereafter in a series of papers. Her most famous find occurred in 1824 when she uncovered the first intact Plesiosaurus skeleton. The specimen was so large and well preserved that it attracted the attention of French zoologist Georges Cuvier, who doubted the finding until he saw the drawings of the specimen in a paper by English geologist and paleontologist William Daniel Conybeare. After Cuvier authenticated the discovery, the scientific community began to recognize the paleontological value of the fossils recovered by Anning and her family.

News of Anning's fossil excavations made her a celebrity and prompted paleontologists, collectors, and tourists to descend on Lyme Regis to buy from her. She went on to recover additional Ichthyosaurus and plesiosaur skeletons from the cliffs. She uncovered a pterosaur in 1828, which became known as Pterodactylus (or Dimorphodon) macronyx. It was the first pterosaur specimen found outside Germany. In 1829 she excavated the skeleton of Squaloraja, a fossil fish thought to be a member of a transition group between sharks and rays.

Anning taught herself geology, anatomy, paleontology, and scientific illustration. Despite her lack of formal scientific training, her discoveries, local area knowledge, and skill at classifying fossils in the field earned her a reputation among paleontology's male and largely upperclass ranks. Her later hunting expeditions sometimes included famous scientists of the time, including British geologist and minister William Buckland and British anatomist and paleontologist Richard Owen, who proposed the term Dinosauria in 1842. She also corresponded with and sold fossils to other leading scientists, such as Cuvier and English geologist Adam Sedgwick.

Nevertheless, Anning was not given full credit for many of the fossils she excavated. Collectors donating specimens to institutions tended to be credited with their discovery. Of the many specimens she found and recovered, several were described in prestigious journals without even a mention of her name. However, some famous scientists of the time, such as British geologist Henry De la Beche and British paleontologist Gideon Mantell, did credit her in their work.

Toward the end of her life, Anning collected annuities from the British Association for the Advancement of Science and the Geological Society of London, which were set up in recognition of her contributions to science. After she died, the president of the Geological Society eulogized her in his annual address, even though the first women would not be admitted to the organization until 1904. In 2010 Anning was recognized by the Royal Society as one of the 10 most influential women scientists in British history. She died on March 9, 1847, in Lyme Regis.

VIRGINIA APGAR

(b. 1909—d. 1974)

Virginia Apgar was an American physician, anesthesiologist, and medical researcher who developed the Apgar Score System, a method of evaluating an infant shortly after birth to assess its well-being and to determine if any immediate medical intervention is required.

Apgar graduated from Mount Holyoke College in 1929 and from the Columbia University College of Physicians and Surgeons in 1933. After an internship at Presbyterian Hospital, New York City, she held residencies in the relatively new specialty of anesthesiology at the University of Wisconsin and then at Bellevue Hospital, New York City, in 1935–37. In 1937 she became the first female board-certified anesthesiologist. The first professor of anesthesiology at the College of Physicians and Surgeons (1949–59), she was also the first female physician to attain the rank of full professor there. Additionally, from 1938 she was director of the department of anesthesiology at Columbia-Presbyterian Medical Center.

An interest in obstetric procedure, and particularly in the treatment of the newborn, led her to develop a simple system for quickly evaluating the condition and viability of newly delivered infants. As finally presented in 1952, the Apgar Score System relies on five simple observations to be made by delivery room personnel (nurses or interns) of the infant within one minute of birth and—depending on the results of the first observation—periodically thereafter. The Apgar Score System soon came into general use throughout the United States and was adopted by several other countries.

In 1959 Apgar left Columbia and took a degree in public health from Johns Hopkins University. She headed the division of congenital malformations at the National Foundation-March of Dimes from 1959-67. She was promoted to director of basic research at the National Foundation (1967-72), and she later became senior vice president for medical affairs (1973-74). She cowrote the book *Is My Baby All Right?* (1972) with Joan Beck.

ANNA ATKINS

(b. 1799—d. 1871)

A nna Atkins, original name Anna Children, was an English photographer and botanist noted for her early use of photography for scientific purposes.

Anna Children, whose mother died soon after she was born, was involved from an early age in the scientific activities that occupied her father, John George Children. A respected scientist, he was secretary of the Royal Society and was associated with the British Museum. While in her early 20s, Atkins made drawings for her father's translation of Jean-Baptiste de Monet Lamarck's *Genera of Shells* (1823), but her prime interest lay in the study of botany. She married John Pelly Atkins in 1825. Through her father's association with Royal Society members William Henry Fox Talbot and the astronomer and chemist Sir John Herschel, Atkins learned of the photographic process then being invented. In particular, she was interested in the cyanotype process devised by Herschel in 1842, which can produce an image by what is commonly called sun-printing. The substance to be recorded is laid on paper impregnated with ferric ammonium citrate and potassium ferricyanide. When exposed to sunlight and then washed in plain water the uncovered areas of the paper turn

8

a rich deep blue. Eventually this process, known as blue-printing, was used mainly to reproduce architectural and engineering drawings.

Atkins employed cyanotype to record all the specimens of algae found in the British Isles. The first part of her work, entitled *British Algae: Cyanotype Impressions*, appeared in 1843, and by 1850 she had produced 12 additional parts. During the next three years Atkins completed the publication with 389 captioned photograms and several pages of text, of which a dozen copies are known. In 1854 Atkins, possibly collaborating with her friend Anne Dixon, produced an album entitled

Ferns, cyanotype by Anna Atkins, 1840s

Cyanotypes of British and Foreign Flowering Plants and Ferns. Despite the simplicity of her means, Atkins's project was the first sustained effort to demonstrate that the medium of photography could be both scientifically useful and aesthetically pleasing.

HERTHA MARKS AYRTON

(b. 1854—d. 1923)

Hertha Marks Ayrton, original name in full Phoebe Sarah Marks, was a British physicist who was the first woman nominated to become a fellow of the Royal Society.

In 1861 Marks's father died, and two years later she went to live with her aunt, author Marion Moss Hartog, who ran a school in London. When she was a teenager, Marks changed her first name to Hertha, after the German earth goddess of Algernon Swinburne's poem *Hertha* (1869), and renounced Judaism to become an agnostic.

In 1876 Marks entered Girton College at the University of Cambridge, where she studied mathematics. There she became a friend of Barbara Bodichon, who had cofounded Girton College, and the writer George Eliot, who based the character of Mirah Cohen in her novel *Daniel Deronda* (1876) on Marks. Cambridge did not offer degrees to women, but Marks did complete her education by taking Cambridge's mathematics examinations, the tripos, in 1881. She then became a teacher of mathematics at high schools in London. In 1884 she invented a type of line divider for use in drafting.

Marks in 1884 attended classes in electricity at Finsbury Technical College that were taught by electrical engineer William Ayrton. They married in 1885. Aside from a series of lectures on electricity to women in 1888, she did not return to science until 1891. In 1893 William was attending a meeting on electricity in Chicago, and in his absence she continued her husband's experiments with the electric arc, which was then used as a lighting source in arc lamps. Electric arcs had a tendency to hiss and sputter before settling down and delivering a consistent light. Ayrton discovered the origin of the hissing in the oxidation of the positive carbon electrode and proposed changes in the shape of the carbon electrodes that greatly reduced the period of hissing.

In 1899 Ayrton read her paper on the hissing of the electric arc to the Institution of Electrical Engineers (IEE). She was the first woman to do so and also became the first woman member of the IEE. That same year she demonstrated her arc experiments at the Conversazione, a public event sponsored by the Royal Society. In 1901, when William was recovering from exhaustion at the seaside town of Margate, Ayrton became interested in the patterns formed by ripples in the sand. She conducted experiments in hydrodynamics to explain the formation of sand ripples. She was nominated to become a fellow of the Royal Society in 1902; however, lawyers advised the Royal Society that its charter would not allow the admission of married women members. Ayrton became the first woman to read a scientific paper (*The Origin and Growth of Ripple-mark*) before the Royal Society in 1904. In 1906 the Royal Society awarded her the Hughes Medal, which is awarded for distinguished work in the physical sciences, for her arc and sand-ripple experiments.

Ayrton became active in the woman suffrage movement, and she joined the Women's Social and Political Union (WSPU) in 1907. She became one of the WSPU's largest contributors; in some years she donated more than £1,000. Suffragettes, such as Emmeline Pankhurst, who had gone on hunger strikes often recuperated at her home. In 1912 Ayrton received £7,000 from the WSPU to forestall government seizure of the WSPU's account. That same year her friend French physicist Marie Curie stayed with her as Curie recovered from a kidney operation.

During World War I Ayrton's interest in hydrodynamics led her to invent a cotton fan that would disperse poison gas from trenches. About 100,000 of the "Ayrton fans" were produced, but they proved ineffective in actual combat conditions. After the war she worked on modified versions of the fan for use by workers in mines and sewers.

FLORENCE AUGUSTA MERRIAM BAILEY

(b. 1863—d. 1948)

Florence Augusta Merriam Bailey, née Florence Augusta Merriam, was an American ornithologist and author of popular field guides.

Florence Merriam was a younger sister of Clinton Hart Merriam, later first chief of the U.S. Biological Survey. She attended private school in Utica, New York, and during 1882—86 she was a student at Smith College, Northampton, Massachusetts; she did not follow a degree course at Smith but was later, in 1921, granted a B.A. Her interest in bird life was already well developed, and a series of articles she wrote for the *Audubon* magazine were later collected in her first book, *Birds Through an Opera Glass* (1889).

Travel and dabblings in social work filled the next few years, but the onset of tuberculosis sent her west to convalesce. Her experiences in Utah, southern California, and Arizona bore fruit in *My Summer in a Mormon Village* (1894), *A-Birding on a Bronco* (1896), and *Birds of Village and Field* (1898). She then took up residence with her brother in Washington, D.C., and in December 1899 married Vernon Bailey, a naturalist with the Biological Survey. Thereafter they shared the life of field naturalists, her energy and enthusiasm enabling her to undertake expeditions on foot or horseback through mountains and across plains.

She continued to publish articles regularly and in 1902 produced her *Handbook of Birds of the Western United States*, a counterpart to Frank M. Chapman's *Handbook of Birds of Eastern North America*. She also contributed to several of her husband's books, notably *Wild Animals of Glacier National Park* (1918) and *Cave Life of Kentucky* (1933). She was a founding member of the Audubon Society of the District of Columbia and frequently led its classes in basic ornithology. She became the first woman associate member of the American Ornithologists' Union in 1885, its first woman fellow in 1929, and the first woman recipient of its Brewster Medal in 1931, awarded for her comprehensive book *Birds of New Mexico* (1928), which she had begun under the auspices of the Biological Survey. Her last major written work was *Among the Birds in the Grand Canyon National Park*, published by the National Park Service in 1939.

A variety of California mountain chickadee was named Parus gambeli baileyae in her honour in 1908.

SARA JOSEPHINE BAKER

(b. 1873—d. 1945)

Sara Josephine Baker was an American physician who contributed significantly to public health and child welfare in the United States.

Baker prepared at private schools for Vassar College, but the death of her father put that school out of reach. She decided to study medicine and after a year of private preparation entered the Women's Medical College of the New York Infirmary in New York City. After graduating in 1898 she interned at the New England Hospital for Women and Children and then entered private practice in New York City.

In 1901 Baker was appointed a medical inspector for the city health department, and in 1907 she became assistant to the commissioner of health. In that post she aided in the apprehension of "Typhoid Mary" Mallon. More importantly, however, she developed from the rudimentary program of inspection for infectious diseases a comprehensive approach to preventive health care for children. In the summer of 1908 she was allowed to test her plan in a slum district on the East Side. A team of 30 nurses under her direction sought out every infant in the district, taught simple hygiene—ventilation, bathing, light clothing, breast-feeding—to the mothers, and made follow-up visits. At the end of the summer the district had recorded 1,200 fewer cases of infant mortality than the previous summer.

In August 1908 the Division of Child Hygiene was established in the health department and Baker was named director. The division (later raised to bureau) was the first government agency in the world devoted to child health. There Baker evolved a broad program including strict examination and licensing of midwives (and from 1911 free instruction at Bellevue Hospital), appointment of school nurses and doctors, compulsory use of silver nitrate drops in the eyes of all newborns, inspection of schoolchildren for infectious diseases, and numerous methods of distributing information on health and hygiene among the poor.

To deal with the inescapable problem faced by working mothers, Baker organized "Little Mothers' Leagues" to provide training to young girls required to care for infants. In 1911 she organized and became president of the Babies Welfare Association; the next year it was reorganized as the Children's Welfare Federation of New York, of which she was president until 1914 and chairman of the executive committee in 1914-17. As a result of her division's work, the infant mortality rate in New York City fell from 144 per 1,000 live births in 1908 to 88 in 1918 and 66 in 1923. By that time the division's health stations were caring for some 60,000 babies a year—half those born in the city. From 1916 to 1930 she lectured on child hygiene at the New York University-Bellevue Hospital Medical School, and in 1917 she was the first woman to receive from it a doctorate in public health. For 16 years, from its organization in 1912, she was a staff consultant to the federal Children's Bureau. After her retirement from the Bureau of Child Hygiene in 1923, she became a consultant to the Children's Bureau and a representative on child health issues to the League of Nations.

In addition to articles in popular and professional journals, Baker published *Healthy Babies, Healthy Children, and Healthy Mothers* (all 1920), *The Growing Child* (1923), *Child Hygiene* (1925), and an autobiography, *Fighting for Life* (1939).

CLARA BARTON

(b. 1821—d. 1912)

The founder of the American branch of the Red Cross was Clara Barton, a nurse who was sometimes called the "angel of the battlefield."

Clara Barton was born on December 25, 1821, in Oxford, Massachusetts. She was christened Clarissa Harlowe by her parents, Stephen and Sarah Barton. Clara was the youngest of seven children, separated by ten years from the next youngest Barton child. Although shy and small, she possessed courage and perseverance. When she was 11 she undertook the nursing of an invalid brother.

To temper Clara's shyness, her mother gave her much responsibility. At 15 Clara became a teacher with her mother's help. She taught school for 18 years. In Bordentown, New Jersey, she persuaded officials to set up a free public school under her direction. When the school proved successful, a male principal was appointed to replace her as head of the staff; Clara resigned her teaching position.

In 1854 she suffered the first of many periods of nervous exhaustion brought on by strenuous work. Later that year she was appointed a clerk in the Patent Office at Washington, D.C. At the outbreak of the Civil War, she learned that much suffering at the front was caused by the scarcity of supplies. Single-handedly she organized supply depots. Later she served as a nurse and, in 1864, was appointed a superintendent of nurses. She often served near the line of fire. For four years after the war she headed the government search for missing soldiers.

While in Europe for her health, Clara Barton studied the action of the Red Cross in the Franco-Prussian War. On her return home in 1872 she campaigned to organize a branch of the Red Cross in the United States. She succeeded in 1881. For 23 years she directed Red Cross work in every great disaster. She resigned in 1904. Clara Barton died on April 12, 1912, in Glen Echo, Maryland.

LAURA BASSI

(b. 1711—d. 1778)

Laura Bassi, in full Laura Maria Catarina Bassi, was an Italian scientist who was the first woman to become a physics professor at a European university.

Bassi was a child prodigy and studied Latin and French. When she was 13, physician Gaetano Tacconi, who was the Bassi family doctor and a professor of medicine and philosophy at the University of Bologna, took charge of her education. In 1731 Tacconi invited philosophers from the university, as well as the archbishop of Bologna, Prospero Cardinal Lambertini, to examine her progress. Lambertini and the philosophers were very impressed. Word quickly spread of Bassi's intelligence, and in 1732 she was at the center of a series of public events organized by Lambertini. On March 20 Bassi was admitted to the Bologna Academy of Sciences as an honorary member, and she was its first female member. On April 17 Bassi defended her theses for the degree of doctor of philosophy. She had became famous in Bologna and thus made her defense in the town hall before Lambertini rather than in the churches of the religious orders, as was customary. Several of her theses showed the influence of Isaac Newton's works on optics and light. On May 12, when Bassi received her degree, the excitement in Bologna over her accomplishments culminated in public celebrations and with collections of poetry published in her honour. On June 27 she defended another set of theses about the properties of water, which led to her being awarded an honorary post at the university as a professor in physics.

In 1738 Bassi married Giovanni Giuseppe Veratti, a physician and also a professor at the university. Because, as a woman, Bassi was not allowed to teach at the university, she gave lectures and experimental demonstrations at her home. She was an early proponent of Newtonian physics and based her courses on material found in Newton's *Principia*. In 1740 Lambertini became Pope Benedict XIV, and in 1745 he reorganized the Bologna Academy of Sciences to create a special group of 25 scientists, called the Benedettini, who were expected to regularly present their research. Bassi lobbied Benedict XIV to become the 25th Benedettini. For a woman to be awarded such an honour was particularly controversial, so Benedict XIV compromised and named Bassi to the Benedettini but without the same voting privileges as the other 24.

In the 1760s Bassi began performing experiments with Veratti on possible medicinal applications of electricity, but she did not publish any papers on the subject. She was appointed to the chair of experimental physics at the University of Bologna in 1776, with Veratti named as her assistant. Bassi thus became the first woman named to a chair of physics at a university.

RUTH BENEDICT

(b. 1887—d. 1948)

U.S. anthropologist Ruth Benedict studied native societies in North America and the South Pacific. Her theories had a profound influence on cultural anthropology, especially in the area of culture and personality.

Benedict was born Ruth Fulton in New York City on June 5, 1887. She graduated from Vassar College in 1909 and taught in girls' schools in California. In 1914 she returned to New York City, and by the early 1920s she entered the field of anthropology, studying under Franz Boas at Columbia University. She received a Ph.D. in 1923 for her thesis on a pervasive theme among North American Indians, The Concept of the Guardian Spirit in North America. In 1924 she began teaching at Columbia. She wrote poetry under the pseudonym Anne Singleton until the early 1930s.

Benedict's first book, *Tales of the Cochiti Indians* (1931), and her two-volume *Zuñi Mythology* (1935) were based on 11 years of fieldwork among and research into the religion and folklore of Native Americans. *Patterns of Culture* (1934), Benedict's major contribution to anthropology, compares Zuñi, Dobu, and Kwakiutl cultures in order to demonstrate how the "personality," the particular complex of traits and attitudes, of a culture defines the individuals within it as successes, misfits, or outcasts. Her other books include *Race: Science and Politics* (1940), an investigation of questions of human equality, and *The Chrysanthemum and the Sword* (1946), an anthropological study of Japan.

From 1943 to 1945 Benedict was a special adviser to the Office of War Information on dealing with the peoples of occupied territories and enemy lands. She returned to Columbia in 1946, and in 1947 she was president of the American Anthropological Association. A few months before her death on Sept. 17, 1948, in New York City, she was named director of a study of contemporary European and Asian cultures.

LOUISE BLANCHARD BETHUNE

(b. 1856—d. 1913)

Louise Blanchard Bethune, née Jennie Louise Blanchard, was the first professional woman architect in the United States.

Louise Blanchard took a position as a draftsman in the Buffalo, New York, architectural firm of Richard A. Waite in 1876. In October 1881 she opened her own architectural office in partnership with Robert A. Bethune, whom she married in December. The firm of R.A. and L. Bethune designed several hundred buildings in Buffalo and throughout New York State, specializing in schools. They also designed hotels, apartment houses, churches, factories, and banks, many of them in the Romanesque Revival style popular in the late 19th century. Among their major commissions were Lockport High School, the East Buffalo Live Stock Exchange, and the Hotel Lafayette in Buffalo (completed in 1904).

In 1885 Bethune joined the Western Association of Architects, of which she later served a term as vice president. She helped organize the Buffalo Society of Architects in 1886; it later became the Buffalo chapter of the American Institute of Architects. She also promoted a licensing law for architects, as well as equal pay for women in the field. In April

Hotel Lafayette, designed by Bethune

1888 she became the first woman elected to membership in the American Institute of Architects, and the next year she became the first woman fellow of the institute.

ELIZABETH H. BLACKBURN

(b. 1948)

Elizabeth H. Blackburn, in full Elizabeth Helen Blackburn, is an Australian-born American molecular biologist and biochemist who was awarded the 2009 Nobel Prize for Physiology or Medicine, along with American molecular biologist Carol W. Greider and American biochemist and geneticist Jack W. Szostak, for her discoveries elucidating the genetic composition and function of telomeres (segments of DNA occurring at the ends of chromosomes) and for her contribution to the discovery of an enzyme called telomerase.

In the early 1970s Blackburn earned a bachelor's and a master's degree in biochemistry from the University of Melbourne. She then enrolled as a graduate student in molecular biology at the University of Cambridge in England, where she worked in the laboratory of British biochemist Frederick Sanger. At Cambridge Blackburn studied the nucleic acid composition of bacteriophage phi X 174 and became familiar with techniques of DNA sequencing. She received a Ph.D. in molecular biology in 1975, and that same year she began her postdoctoral research in the laboratory of American cell biologist and geneticist Joseph Gall, at Yale University in New Haven, Conn. Gall's research was concerned primarily with the structure and replication of chromosomes, and Blackburn followed his lead, investigating the chromosomes of a protozoan called Tetrahymena. She sequenced the DNA of the organism's telomeres and thereby discovered that telomeres are composed of short repeating segments of DNA.

In 1978 Blackburn became an assistant professor of molecular biology at the University of California, Berkeley, and continued her investigations of the telomeres of Tetrahymena. She became increasingly interested in the function and maintenance of the repeated segments of DNA that make up the ends of chromosomes. In 1980 Blackburn met Szostak, who was also

Elizabeth H. Blackburn

studying telomeres and who was intrigued by Blackburn's research. The two began a collaborative effort to understand telomere function, using both yeast and Tetrahymena as model organisms for their investigations. In 1984 Blackburn and Greider, who was then a graduate student in Blackburn's laboratory, discovered telomerase. Their subsequent studies revealed that telomerase plays a fundamental role in maintaining chromosomes because it can add DNA to telomeres, which shorten following cell division and are the primary determinants of cell life span.

Blackburn remained at Berkeley until 1990, when she became a professor in the department of biochemistry and biophysics and in the department of microbiology and immunology at the University of California, San Francisco (UCSF). In 1993 she earned the additional title of chair of the department of microbiology and immunology at UCSF. Blackburn's later research involved further investigation of the genetic composition and cellular functions of telomeres and telomerase, as well as studies on the interactions of these cellular components and their roles in cancer and aging.

Throughout her career Blackburn published a number of scientific papers and received a variety of honorary degrees and awards, including the Gairdner Foundation International Award (1998; shared with Greider), the Lewis S. Rosenstiel Award for Distinguished Work in Basic Medical Science (1999; shared with Greider), and the Albert Lasker Basic Medical Research Award (2006; shared with Greider and Szostak). Blackburn also was elected a fellow of the Royal Society of London (1992) and a Foreign Associate of the National Academy of Sciences (1993).

ELIZABETH BLACKWELL

(b. 1821—d. 1910)

When Elizabeth Blackwell was graduated as a doctor of medicine in 1849, she became the first woman doctor in the United States. Her enrollment in the Medical Register of the United Kingdom in 1859 made her Europe's first modern woman doctor.

Elizabeth was born on Feb. 3, 1821, in Bristol, England. She was one

Elizabeth Blackwell

of nine children of Samuel Blackwell, a prosperous sugar refiner. The Blackwells immigrated to New York City in 1832. There the family was active in the abolitionist movement. Their refinery unfortunately did not prosper, and in 1838 they moved to Cincinnati, Ohio. Samuel Blackwell died a few months after the move. The need for the boys to find work and the girls to start school did not prevent the Blackwells from aiding escaped slaves or from participating in intellectual movements.

It was in 1844 that slight, yellow-haired Elizabeth Blackwell determined to become a doctor. Because no medical school would admit her, she studied privately with doctors in the South and in Philadelphia. In 1847 the Geneva Medical School of western New York accepted her. The acceptance evoked a storm of ridicule and criticism, but in spite of slights and embarrassments Elizabeth pursued her studies. In 1849 she was graduated at the head of her class.

Paris then was the foremost medical center. Dr. Blackwell journeyed there to undertake advanced studies, but Paris doctors proved as intolerant as their American colleagues. They would not permit her to study as a doctor. She was forced to enter a large maternity hospital as a student midwife. There she contracted an infection that caused her to lose her sight in one eye. After convalescence, she went to London, where she was permitted to continue her studies.

On her return to New York City in 1850, Dr. Blackwell was not permitted to practice in any hospital. Dr. Blackwell fought for her own and other women's rights to learn and practice. She started the New York Infirmary for Women and Children, aided by her sister Emily and other women who became doctors and by several tolerant Quakers. Her leadership in meeting the medical problems presented by the Civil War won her recognition. With her sister she opened a medical college for women in her hospital.

Dr. Blackwell wrote and lectured. A series of lectures which she delivered in England in 1859 brought her recognition in Britain. After the Civil War she settled in England. Her work and her friendship with Florence Nightingale and other intellectual leaders of the day opened the way for English women to enter the field of medicine.

Her lectures and books dealt largely with social hygiene and with preventive medicine. She died May 31, 1910, at her home in Hastings, England.

EMILY BLACKWELL

(b. 1826—d. 1910)

Physician, teacher, and administrator Emily Blackwell contributed greatly to the education and acceptance of women medical professionals in the United States. Along with her sister Elizabeth, who was the first licensed woman physician in modern times, Blackwell ran the New York Infirmary for Women and Children (now NYU Downtown Hospital).

Emily Blackwell was born on Oct. 8, 1826, in Bristol, England, to an affluent and cultivated family. Like her sister, she was well educated by private tutors. She grew up in the United States, in New York City, in Jersey City, N.J., and in Cincinnati, Ohio. In 1848, following her sister's example, she began studying medicine. Because of her gender, she was rejected by several medical schools, including the Geneva (New York) Medical College, which had accepted Elizabeth but then reversed its policy on admitting women. In 1852–53 Emily attended Rush Medical College in Chicago until outside pressures led the school to dismiss her. At last she gained admittance to the medical college of Western Reserve University in Cleveland, Ohio, from which she graduated in March 1854. She subsequently pursued further studies in Edinburgh, Scotland, under James Young Simpson, in London, England, under William Jenner, and in Paris, France, and Berlin and Dresden, Germany.

In 1856 she settled in New York City and worked in her sister's dispensary, which the next year became the New York Infirmary for Women and Children. From the beginning of that association, Emily Blackwell took responsibility for infirmary management and in large part for fundraising. She also served as chief of surgery. The infirmary grew steadily. In-home medical social work was subsequently undertaken, followed by a program of nurses' training that began in 1858. The Women's Medical College, a full medical school, was in operation by 1868.

In 1869, when her sister moved to England, Blackwell became the sole administrator of the infirmary and school. As dean of the college as well as professor of obstetrics and the diseases of women, she oversaw the growth of the college into a four-year institution in 1893. In this extent of training, the Women's Medical College was ahead of much of the profession, as it had been in 1876 in instituting a three-year course. By 1899 the college had graduated 364 women. In that year Blackwell transferred her students to Cornell University Medical College, which had begun accepting men and women students on an equal basis. She continued her work with the infirmary until her death, on Sept. 7, 1910, in York Cliffs, Maine.

ELIZABETH GERTRUDE KNIGHT BRITTON

(b. 1858—d. 1934)

Elizabeth Gertrude Knight Britton, née Elizabeth Gertrude Knight, was an American botanist known for her lasting contributions to the study of mosses.

Elizabeth Knight grew up for the most part in Cuba, where her family owned a sugar plantation. She attended schools in Cuba and New York and in 1875 graduated from Normal (now Hunter) College, New York City. For 10 years she worked on the staff there, and during that time she laid the foundation of her reputation as a leading amateur botanist. By 1883 she had specialized in bryology, the study of mosses, and had published her first scientific paper in the field.

In August 1885 she married Nathaniel L. Britton, a geologist at Columbia College (now Columbia University) in New York City. He soon turned to botany, and over the next several years the two made numerous field trips together to the West Indies. She was given charge, on an unofficial basis, of the moss collection of the Columbia botany department, and gradually she built an impressive collection, notably with the purchase of the collection of August Jaeger of Switzerland in 1893. In 1886–88 she was editor of the *Bulletin of the Torrey Botanical Club,* of which she had been a member since 1879. Supported by the Torrey Botanical Club and other interested persons, the Brittons took

25

the lead in urging the establishment of a botanical garden in New York. The New York Botanical Garden was incorporated in 1891, and in 1896 Nathaniel Britton became first director of the 250-acre (100-hectare; from 1915, nearly 400-acre [160-hectare]) establishment in Bronx Park. The Columbia College herbarium was transferred there in 1899, and Elizabeth Britton became unofficial curator of mosses. In 1912 she received appointment as honorary curator of mosses.

In 1902 Britton was a founder and in 1902-16 and 1918-27 secretary and treasurer of the Wild Flower Preservation Society of America. Through the society and various publications she led movements that succeeded in saving numerous endangered wildflower species around the country. From 1916 to 1919 she was president of the Sullivant Moss Society, which she had helped found in 1898 and which in 1949 became the American Bryological Society. She published more than 340 signed scientific papers during her career and had 15 species and 1 moss genus (*Bryobrittonia*) named for her.

LINDA B. BUCK

(b. 1947—d.)

Linda B. Buck is an American scientist and corecipient, with Richard Axel, of the Nobel Prize for Physiology or Medicine in 2004 for discoveries concerning the olfactory system.

Buck received a B.S. (1975) in both microbiology and psychology from the University of Washington and a Ph.D. (1980) in immunology from the University of Texas Southwestern Medical Center. She first worked with Axel in the early 1980s at Columbia University in New York City, where Axel was a professor and Buck was his postdoctoral student. Buck held various positions with the Howard Hughes Medical Institute (HHMI) and at Harvard Medical School from 1984 until 2002, when she joined the Fred Hutchinson Cancer Research Center in Seattle.

In 1991 Buck and Axel jointly published a landmark scientific paper, based on research they had conducted with laboratory rats, that detailed their discovery of the family of 1,000 genes that encode, or produce,

Linda B. Buck receiving the Nobel Prize

an equivalent number of olfactory receptors. These receptors are proteins responsible for detecting the odorant molecules in the air and are located on olfactory receptor cells, which are clustered within a small area in the back of the nasal cavity. The two scientists then clarified how the olfactory system functions by showing that each receptor cell has only one type of odour receptor, which is specialized to recognize a few odours. After odorant molecules bind to receptors, the receptor cells send electrical signals to the olfactory bulb in the brain. The brain combines information from several types of receptors in specific patterns, which are experienced as distinct odours.

Axel and Buck later determined that most of the details they uncovered about the sense of smell are virtually identical in rats, humans, and other animals, although they discovered that humans have only about

350 types of working olfactory receptors, about one-third the number in rats. Nevertheless, the genes that encode olfactory receptors in humans account for about 3 percent of all human genes. The work helped boost scientific interest in the possible existence of human pheromones, odorant molecules known to trigger sexual activity and certain other behaviour in many animals, and Buck's HHMI laboratory carried on research into how odour perceptions are translated into emotional responses and instinctive behaviour.

JOCELYN BELL BURNELL

(b. 1943)

British astronomer Jocelyn Bell Burnell discovered pulsars, the cosmic sources of peculiar radio pulses.

Bell Burnell was born July 15, 1943, in Belfast, Northern Ireland. She attended the University of Glasgow, Scotland, where she received a bachelor's degree (1965) in physics. She proceeded to the University of Cambridge, England, where she was awarded a doctorate (1969) in radioastronomy. As a research assistant at Cambridge, she aided in constructing a large radio telescope and in 1967, while reviewing the printouts of her experiments monitoring quasars, discovered a series of extremely regular radio pulses. Puzzled, she consulted her adviser, astrophysicist Antony Hewish, and their team spent the ensuing months eliminating possible sources of the pulses, which they jokingly dubbed LGM (for Little Green Men) in reference to the remote possibility that they represented attempts at communication by extraterrestrial intelligence. After monitoring the pulses using more sensitive equipment, the team discovered several more regular patterns of radio waves and determined that they were in fact emanating from rapidly spinning neutron stars (pulsating radio stars), which were later called pulsars by the press.

The 1974 Nobel Prize for Physics was awarded to Hewish and Martin Ryle for the discovery of pulsars. Several prominent scientists protested the omission of Bell Burnell, though she maintained that the prize was

28

presented appropriately given her student status at the time of the discovery. Subsequent to her discovery, Bell Burnell taught at the University of Southampton (1970—73) before becoming a professor at University College London (1974—82). She also taught at the Open University (1973—87) and worked at the Royal Observatory in Edinburgh (1982—91) before serving as professor of physics at the Open University (1991—2001). Bell Burnell was then appointed dean of science at the University of Bath (2001—04), after which she accepted a post as visiting professor at Oxford University, England.

Bell Burnell was created Commander of the Order of the British Empire (CBE) in 1999 and Dame (DBE) in 2007. Bell Burnell became a member of the British Royal Society in 2003. She also served as president of the Royal Astronomical Society (2002—04) and was elected to a two-year term as president of the Institute of Physics in 2008.

ANNIE JUMP CANNON

(b. 1863—d. 1941)

Known as the "census taker of the sky," U.S. astronomer Annie Jump Cannon developed the Harvard system of classifying stars. Her method involved studying the spectra, or properties of light, emitted by the stars.

Cannon was born in Dover, Del., on Dec. 11, 1863. After attending Wellesley and Radcliffe colleges, she joined the staff of the Harvard College observatory and worked there for the rest of her life.

Using her system of spectral classification by surface temperature, she demonstrated that the vast majority of stars can be grouped into only a few types and those types can be arranged into a continuous series. She measured and classified spectra for more than 225,300 stars of ninth magnitude or brighter. Her work was published in *The Henry Draper Catalogue* from 1918 to 1924.

In addition to classifying thousands of stars Cannon also discovered more than 300 variable stars and five novas. The first woman ever awarded an honorary doctorate by Oxford University, Cannon continued her research until her death at Cambridge, Mass., on April 13, 1941.

RACHEL CARSON
(b. 1907—d. 1964)

Drawing on her childhood fascination with wildlife and the sea, American biologist Rachel Carson became a scientific writer whose works appeal to a wide range of readers. Her enchanting book *The Sea Around Us*, published in 1951, was a best-seller and the winner of a National Book Award. Her prophetic work *Silent Spring* (1962), about the dangers of pesticides in the food chain, created worldwide awareness of the dangers of pollution.

Rachel Louise Carson was born on May 27, 1907, in Springdale, Pa. She did her undergraduate work at the Pennsylvania College for Women, where she received her B.A. in 1929. She then went on to earn an M.A. from Johns Hopkins University in 1932. From 1931 to 1936 she taught zoology at the University of Maryland. During this period she also taught in the Johns Hopkins summer school and studied at the Marine Biological Laboratory in Woods Hole, Mass.

Carson accepted a position in 1936 as an aquatic biologist with the United States Bureau of Fisheries (from 1940 called the U.S. Fish and Wildlife Service). She would hold this government post for the next 16 years. From 1949 to 1952 she served as editor in chief of the Fish and Wildlife Service's publications. By that time Carson had become widely known as a science writer. Her first three books were about sea life: *Under the Sea-Wind* (1941), *The Sea Around Us*, and *The Edge of the Sea* (1955) displayed Carson's remarkable talent for combining scientific observation with elegant and lyrical prose descriptions.

After the publication of *The Edge of the Sea*, Carson spent much of the next five years conducting research for *Silent Spring*. The book, which detailed the harmful effects that pesticides such as DDT had on the environment—and particularly on wildlife—became her second best-seller and today is regarded as a landmark work in the history of the modern environmental movement. Carson died on April 14, 1964.

MARGARET CHAN

(b. 1947)

Margaret Chan is a Hong Kong–born Chinese civil servant who became director general of the World Health Organization (WHO) in January 2007.

Chan attended Northcote College of Education in Hong Kong before moving to Canada, where she earned B.A. (1973) and M.D. (1977) degrees from the University of Western Ontario. She also received a Master of Science degree in public health (1985) from Singapore National University. She joined the Hong Kong Department of Health in 1978 and became its director in 1994. She served as director for nine years, during which time she focused on communicable disease surveillance and response and on improving training for public health professionals.

Chan's leadership during a time of crisis was widely commended after the first human cases of the deadly H5N1 bird flu virus appeared in Hong Kong in 1997. Her response included an order to destroy the city's entire poultry stock—some 1.5 million birds. The order, carried out within three days, allowed authorities to bring the outbreak under control and possibly avert a pandemic. Chan also elevated her international profile with her management of the 2003 SARS outbreak, which claimed the lives of nearly 300 persons in Hong Kong, though some critics faulted her for not acting more aggressively after the outbreak initially appeared in China's neighbouring Guangdong province.

From 2003 to 2005 Chan served as director of WHO's Department of Protection of the Human Environment, and from 2005 until 2007 she was WHO's assistant director general for communicable diseases. Chan succeeded Lee Jong Wook of South Korea as director general of WHO a few months after his unexpected death. She and 10 other candidates were recommended for the post by their respective governments, and, after four rounds of balloting by WHO's executive board, Chan emerged as the nominee. Her selection was confirmed during a special session of the World Health Assembly on November 9. Supporters praised Chan's ability in handling crisis situations, pointing to her experience in managing the bird flu and SARS outbreaks.

Chan officially became director general in early January 2007. In her first speech after taking the position, she outlined her specific goals of improving the health of people in Africa and of women around the world. "All regions, all countries, all people are equally important," she stated, "but we must focus our attention on the people in greatest need." In 2009, during an ongoing outbreak of swine flu that began in Mexico and subsequently spread to countries worldwide, Chan was confronted with the difficult task of assessing the potential global health impact of the disease. On June 11, 2009, following a series of meetings with an emergency committee from whom she sought scientific evidence on which to base her decision, Chan officially declared the swine flu outbreak a pandemic. It was the first pandemic to be declared since 1968.

GABRIELLE-ÉMILIE CHÂTELET
(b. 1706—d. 1749)

In her lifetime, Gabrielle-Émilie Châtelet attracted attention in France for her romantic relationships with various intellectuals, particularly Voltaire. Today she is remembered as a mathematician and physicist who championed Sir Isaac Newton's scientific theories.

Gabrielle-Émilie Le Tonnelier de Breteuil was born on Dec. 17, 1706, in Paris. As a child she showed such intelligence that her aristocratic father hired tutors for her. At age 19 she married a soldier, but she saw her husband infrequently. She preferred the company of scientists and mathematicians. In 1733 she met Voltaire, a leading thinker and writer. The following year he moved into the Châtelet estate in Cirey, which the two made into a hub of literary and scientific activity.

Châtelet's best-known work is her translation from Latin into French, with commentary, of Newton's *Principia Mathematica*, which set forth his theory of gravity. It was published in 1759, after Châtelet's death from childbirth complications in Lunéville, France, on Sept. 10, 1749. Her other writings include a paper on the nature of fire (1744) and a work on physics (1740), which helped to spread the theories of the German mathematician Gottfried Leibniz.

CORNELIA MARIA CLAPP

(b. 1849—d. 1934)

Cornelia Maria Clapp was an American zoologist and educator whose influence as a teacher was great and enduring in a period when the world of science was just opening to women.

Clapp graduated from Mount Holyoke Female Seminary in 1871, and after a year of teaching elsewhere she returned to Mount Holyoke as an instructor in mathematics. Later she also taught gymnastics. Her budding interest in natural history was encouraged when, in 1874, she was selected to attend the summer Anderson School of Natural History conducted by Louis Agassiz at Penikese Island in Buzzards Bay, Massachusetts. Soon Clapp was teaching zoology at Mount Holyoke, where she developed a vivid laboratory method of instruction that proved highly effective. She continued her own education on numerous field trips and in formal studies at the Massachusetts Institute of Technology in Cambridge, at Williams College in Williamstown, Massachusetts, at Syracuse (New York) University, where she received a Ph.D. degree in 1889, and at the University of Chicago, where she took a second doctorate in 1896.

In 1896, eight years after Mount Holyoke became a college, Clapp helped organize the department of zoology, and in 1904 she was named professor of zoology. From its opening in 1888 she was involved in the work of the Marine Biological Laboratory at Woods Hole, Massachusetts. She carried on research there, primarily in the field of embryology, and served as librarian in 1893—1907 and as a trustee in 1897—1901 and again in 1910. She retired as professor emeritus from Mount Holyoke in 1916 but continued for several years to summer at Woods Hole. She published little during her career, her major influence being to extend scientific knowledge and opportunity to women through education. In 1923 Clapp Hall, housing the science departments and laboratories, was dedicated at Mount Holyoke.

JOHNNETTA COLE

(b. 1936)

Johnnetta Cole is an anthropologist and educator who was the first African American woman president of Spelman College (1987–97).

Among Cole's early influences in education were her mother, who taught college English, pioneering educator Mary MacLeod Bethune, and writer Arna Bontemps, who was the school librarian at Fisk University when Cole matriculated at age 15. She left Fisk to study sociology at Oberlin College (B.A., 1957) and anthropology at Northwestern University (M.A., 1959; Ph.D., 1967).

After teaching at the University of California, Los Angeles (1964), and directing the black studies program at Washington State University at Pullman (1969–70), Cole taught in the anthropology department at the University of Massachusetts at Amherst (1970–83), where from 1981 to 1983 she was provost of undergraduate education. A pivotal figure in the development of the school's African American Studies program, she became closely associated with the academic journal Black Scholar. In 1983 she moved to Hunter College, where she directed the Latin American and Caribbean Studies program.

In 1987 Cole became the seventh president of Spelman College, the oldest African American women's college in the United States. She was committed to making the school a centre for scholarship about African American women. Calling herself "Sister President," she became known as a strong advocate for the liberal arts curriculum in a changing society. She retired as president emerita in 1997.

In 1998 Cole returned to teaching as Presidential Distinguished Professor of Anthropology, Women's Studies, and African American Studies at Emory University, retiring in 2001. From 2002 to 2007 she was president of Bennett College for Women, where she chaired the Johnnetta B. Cole Global Diversity & Inclusion Institute. She also served as member (2004–) and chair (2004–06) of the board of trustees of the United Way of America, a nationwide network of charitable and community organizations. In February 2009 Cole was named director of the Smithsonian Institution's National Museum of African Art.

Cole's writings focus on race, gender, and class in the pan-African world. In addition to many scholarly articles and a regular column in *McCall's* magazine, she wrote *Anthropology for the Eighties: Introductory Readings* (1982), *All American Women: Lines That Divide, Ties That Bind* (1986), *Anthropology for the Nineties* (1988), *Conversations: Straight Talk with America's Sister President* (1993), and *Dream the Boldest Dreams: And Other Lessons of Life* (1997).

EILEEN COLLINS

(b. 1956)

Eileen Collins is an American astronaut, the first woman to pilot and, later, to command a U.S. space shuttle.

Collins's love of airplanes and flying began as a child. At age 19 she saved money earned from part-time jobs and began taking flying lessons. She graduated with a bachelor's degree in mathematics and economics from Syracuse (New York) University in 1978. She then became one of four women admitted to Air Force Undergraduate Pilot Training at Vance Air Force Base in Oklahoma. The first women astronauts were doing their parachute training at the same base at that time, and Collins realized that the goal of becoming an astronaut was within reach. In 1979 she became the Air Force's first female flight instructor and for the next 11 years taught both flying and math. As a C-141 Starlifter transport aircraft commander, Collins participated in the U.S.-led invasion of Grenada in 1983, delivering troops and evacuating medical students. She continued her training at the Air Force's Institute of Technology and was one of the first women to attend Air Force Test Pilot School, from which she graduated in 1990. She eventually achieved the Air Force rank of colonel. She also earned an M.S. in operations research from Stanford University in 1986 and an M.A.

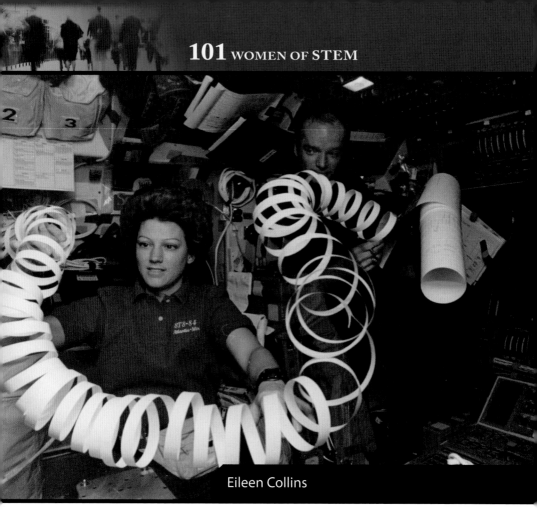

Eileen Collins

in space systems management from Webster University, St. Louis, Missouri, in 1989.

Selected as an astronaut in 1990, Collins became the first woman pilot of a U.S. space shuttle in February 1995, serving on the orbiter *Discovery* for a rendezvous and docking mission to the Russian space station Mir. She piloted a second shuttle flight in May 1997, successfully docking the *Atlantis* with Mir to transfer personnel, equipment, and supplies. With hundreds of hours in space to her credit, Collins became the first woman to command a shuttle mission in July 1999, taking *Columbia* into Earth orbit to deploy the Chandra X-ray Observatory. After *Columbia* was destroyed on a subsequent flight in February 2003, the entire shuttle fleet was grounded until July 2005, when Collins commanded *Discovery* on a "return to flight" mission to test new safety modifications and to resupply the International Space Station (ISS). Prior to *Discovery*'s docking with the ISS, Collins guided the spacecraft through a full 360° pitch (nose-over-tail) maneuver—the first person to do so with an orbiter—which allowed ISS crew members to photograph the spacecraft's belly for possible damage.

ANNA BOTSFORD COMSTOCK

(b. 1854—d. 1930)

U.S. illustrator, writer, and educator Anna Botsford Comstock was a naturalist and wood engraver. She worked both separately and with her husband, entomologist John Henry Comstock, to produce several important works on nature study.

Anna Botsford was born on Sept. 1, 1854, near the town of Otto in Cattaraugus county, N.Y. She entered Cornell University in Ithaca, N.Y., in 1874, but she left after two years. In 1878 she married Comstock, a young entomologist on the Cornell faculty who stoked her interest in insect illustration. Throughout their marriage she functioned as his assistant, illustrating his lectures and publications on insects. Her work was usually on an informal, unpaid basis, but when he was chief entomologist in the U.S. Department of Agriculture (1879 – 81), she received a formal appointment. There she prepared the drawings for his *Report of the Entomologist* (on citrus scale insects) of 1880. She then reentered Cornell and took a degree in natural history in 1885. Thereafter she studied wood engraving at Cooper Union, New York City, in order to prepare illustrations for her husband's *Introduction to Entomology* (1888), and in 1888 she was one of the first four women admitted to Sigma Xi, a national honor society for the sciences.

Comstock made engravings for the more than 600 plates in her husband's *Manual for the Study of Insects* (1895) and for *Insect Life* (1897) and *How to Know the Butterflies* (1904), both of which she co-authored. Her engravings were also widely exhibited and won several prizes. Books that she both wrote and illustrated include *Ways of the Six-Footed* (1903), *How to Keep Bees* (1905), *The Handbook of Nature Study* (1911, with more than two dozen editions), *The Pet Book* (1914), and *Trees at Leisure* (1916).

In 1895 Comstock was appointed to the New York State Committee for the Promotion of Agriculture. While on the committee, she planned and conducted an experimental course of nature study for public schools. When the program was approved for statewide use through the extension service of Cornell, she wrote and spoke on its behalf, helped train teachers, and prepared classroom materials. From 1897 she taught nature study at Cornell.

Comstock lectured frequently to teachers' and farmers' institutes and at universities. She was editor of the journal *Nature-Study Review* (1917—23) and was on the staff of the magazine *Country Life in America*. She also wrote a novel, *Confessions to a Heathen Idol* (1906). In 1922 she retired from Cornell as professor emerita but continued to teach in the summer session. Comstock died on Aug. 24, 1930, in Ithaca, N.Y.

GERTY CORI

(b. 1896—d. 1984)

Gerty Cori was an American biochemist, who, along with her husband, Carl Cori, discovered a phosphate-containing form of the simple sugar glucose. Its universal importance to carbohydrate metabolism led to an understanding of hormonal influence on the interconversion of sugars and starches in the animal organism. Their discoveries earned them (with Bernardo Houssay) the Nobel Prize for Medicine or Physiology in 1947.

They met while students at the German University of Prague and were married in 1920, receiving their medical degrees the same year. Immigrating to the United States in 1922, they joined the staff of the Institute for the Study of Malignant Disease, Buffalo, N.Y. (1922-31). As faculty members of the Washington University medical school, St. Louis (from 1931), they discovered (1936) the activated intermediate, glucose 1-phosphate (phosphate bound to a specific carbon atom on the glucose molecule), known as the "Cori ester." They demonstrated that it represents the first step in the conversion into glucose of the animal storage carbohydrate glycogen, large quantities of which are found in the liver, and—because the reaction is reversible—in some cases the last step in the conversion of blood glucose to glycogen.

Six years later they isolated and purified the enzyme (glycogen phosphorylase) responsible for catalyzing the glycogen-Cori ester reaction, and with it they achieved the test-tube synthesis of glycogen in 1943. Proof of the interconversion allowed them to formulate the "Cori cycle," postulating that liver glycogen is converted to blood glucose that is reconverted to glycogen in muscle, where its breakdown to lactic acid provides the energy utilized in muscle contraction. The lactic acid is used to re-form glycogen in the liver. Studying the way in which hormones affect carbohydrate metabolism in animals, the Coris showed that epinephrine induces the formation of a type of phosphorylase enzyme favouring conversion of glycogen to activated glucose and that insulin causes the removal of sugar from the blood by promoting the addition of phosphate to glucose. The Coris trained a large number of graduate students and postdoctoral fellows from all over the world.

ELENA CORNARO

(b. 1646—d. 1684)

Elena Cornaro was an Italian savant who was the first woman to receive a degree from a university.

Cornaro's father, Giovanni Battista Cornaro Piscopia, was a nobleman. Her mother, Zanetta Boni, was a peasant and was not married to Giovanni (by whom she had four other children) at the time of Elena's birth. When Elena was seven, a friend of her family, the priest Giovanni Fabris, encouraged her father to begin lessons for her in Greek and Latin. She later became fluent in French, Spanish, and Hebrew, and she also studied mathematics, astronomy, philosophy, music, and theology. In 1669 she translated from Spanish into Italian *Colloquio di Cristo nostro Redentore all'anima devota* ("Dialogue between Christ Our Redeemer and a Devoted Soul"), a book by the Carthusian monk Giovanni Laspergio. The fame of her intellectual accomplishment spread, and she was invited to join several scholarly societies. In 1670 she became president of the Venetian society Accademia dei Pacifici (the Academy of the Peaceful).

In 1672—upon the recommendation of Carlo Rinaldini, her tutor in philosophy—Felice Rotondi, her tutor in theology, petitioned the University of Padua to grant Cornaro the degree of doctor of theology. Gregorio Cardinal Barbarigo, the bishop of Padua, assumed that Cornaro was seeking a degree in philosophy and supported her pursuit of a degree. However, when he discovered that Cornaro sought a degree in theology, he refused to grant her the degree because she was a woman. He did allow her to pursue a doctor of philosophy degree, however. On June 25, 1678, because of the immense interest in Cornaro, her defense was held in the cathedral of Padua rather than at the university. Cornaro's defense, which consisted of explaining two passages chosen at random from Aristotle, was successful, and she was presented with the traditional laurel wreath, ermine cape, gold ring, and book of philosophy.

Cornaro had become an oblate (lay monastic) in the Benedictine order in 1665, and after receiving her degree she divided her time between further studies and ministering to the poor. She was in poor health for much of her life, and the extensive charitable work, the rigorous penances she performed, and her extreme dedication to her studies took their toll on her weak physical condition. Her death in 1684 was marked by memorial services in Venice, Padua, Siena, and Rome.

MARIE CURIE

(b. 1867—d. 1934)

Polish-born French physicist Marie Curie was famous for her work on radioactivity and twice a winner of the Nobel Prize. With Henri Becquerel and her husband, Pierre Curie, she was awarded the 1903 Nobel Prize for Physics. She was the sole winner of the 1911 Nobel Prize for Chemistry. Marie Curie was the first woman to win a Nobel Prize, and she is the only woman to win the award in two different fields.

Maria Salomea Sklodowska was born on November 7, 1867, in Warsaw, in what was then the Congress Kingdom of Poland, Russian Empire. From childhood she was remarkable for her prodigious memory, and at the age of 16 she won a gold medal on completion of her secondary education at the Russian lycée. Because her father, a teacher of mathematics and physics, lost his savings through bad investment, she had to take work as a teacher and at the same time took part clandestinely in the nationalist "free university," reading in Polish to women workers. At the age of 18 she took a post as a governess, where she suffered an unhappy love affair. However, from her earnings she was able to finance her sister Bronislawa's medical studies in Paris, France, with the understanding that Bronislawa would in turn later help her to get an education.

In 1891 Sklodowska went to Paris and—now using the name Marie—began to follow the lectures of Paul Appel, Gabriel Lippmann, and Edmond Bouty at the Sorbonne university. Sklodowska worked far into the night and completed degrees in physics and math. It was in the spring of 1891 that she met Pierre Curie.

Their marriage (July 25, 1895) marked the start of a partnership that was soon to achieve results of world significance, in particular the discovery of polonium (so called by Marie in honor of her native land) in the summer of 1898 and that of radium a few months later. Following Henri Becquerel's discovery (1896) of a new phenomenon (which she later called "radioactivity"), Marie Curie, looking for a subject for a thesis, decided to find out if the property discovered in uranium was to be found in other matter. She discovered that this was true for thorium at the same time as Gerhard Carl Schmidt did.

Turning her attention to minerals, she found her interest drawn to pitchblende. Pitchblende, a mineral whose activity is superior to that of pure uranium, could be explained only by the presence in the ore of small quantities of an unknown substance of very high activity. Pierre Curie then joined Marie in the work that she had undertaken to resolve this problem and that led to the discovery of the new elements, polonium and radium. While Pierre Curie devoted himself chiefly to the physical study of the new radiations, Marie Curie struggled to obtain pure radium in the metallic state—achieved with the help of the chemist André-Louis Debierne, one of Pierre Curie's pupils. On the results of this research,

Marie Curie received her doctorate of science in June 1903 and—with Pierre—was awarded the Davy Medal of the Royal Society. Also in 1903 they shared with Becquerel the Nobel Prize for Physics for the discovery of radioactivity.

The birth of her two daughters, Irène and Ève, in 1897 and 1904, did not interrupt Marie's intensive scientific work. She was appointed lecturer in physics (1900) at the École Normale Supérieure for girls in Sèvres, France, and introduced there a method of teaching based on experimental demonstrations. In December 1904 she was appointed chief assistant in the laboratory directed by Pierre Curie.

The sudden death of Pierre Curie (April 19, 1906) was a bitter blow to Marie Curie, but it was also a decisive turning point in her career: henceforth she was to devote all her energy to completing alone the scientific work that they had undertaken. On May 13, 1906, she was appointed to the professorship that had been left vacant on her husband's death; she was the first woman to teach in the Sorbonne. In 1908 she became titular professor, and in 1910 her fundamental treatise on radioactivity was published. In 1911 she was awarded the Nobel Prize for Chemistry, for the isolation of pure radium. In 1914 she saw the completion of the building of the laboratories of the Radium Institute (Institut du Radium) at the University of Paris.

Throughout World War I, Marie Curie, with the help of her daughter Irène, devoted herself to the development of the use of X-radiography. In 1918 the Radium Institute, the staff of which Irène had joined, began to operate in earnest, and it was to become a universal center for nuclear physics and chemistry. Marie Curie, now at the highest point of her fame and, from 1922, a member of the Academy of Medicine, devoted her researches to the study of the chemistry of radioactive substances and the medical applications of these substances.

In 1921, accompanied by her two daughters, Marie Curie made a triumphant journey to the United States, where President Warren G. Harding presented her with a gram of radium that had been bought as the result of a collection among American women. Curie gave lectures, especially in Belgium, Brazil, Spain, and Czechoslovakia. She was made a member of the International Commission on Intellectual Co-operation by the Council of the League of Nations. In addition, she had the satisfaction of seeing the development of the Curie Foundation in Paris and in Poland the inauguration in 1932 in Warsaw of the Radium Institute, of which her sister Bronislawa became director.

One of Marie Curie's outstanding achievements was to have understood the need to accumulate intense radioactive sources, not only to treat illness but also to maintain an abundant supply for research in nuclear physics; the resultant stockpile was an unrivaled instrument until the appearance after 1930 of particle accelerators. The existence in Paris at the Radium Institute of a stock of 1.5 grams of radium in which, over a period of several years, radium D and polonium had accumulated made a decisive contribution to the success of the experiments undertaken in the years around 1930 — in particular of those experiments performed by Irène Curie in conjunction with Frédéric Joliot, whom she had married in 1926. This work prepared the way for the discovery of the neutron by Sir James Chadwick and, above all, for the discovery in 1934 by Irène and Frédéric Joliot-Curie of artificial radioactivity. A few months after this discovery, Marie Curie died as a result of leukemia caused by the action of radiation. Her contribution to physics had been immense, not only in her own work, the importance of which had been demonstrated by the award to her of two Nobel Prizes, but because of her influence on subsequent generations of nuclear physicists and chemists. Marie Curie, together with Irène Joliot-Curie, wrote the entry on radium for the 13th edition (1926) of the *Encyclopædia Britannica*.

Marie Curie died on July 4, 1934, near Sallanches, France. In 1995 her ashes were enshrined in the Panthéon in Paris; she was the first woman to receive this honor for her own achievements. Her office and laboratory in the Curie Pavilion of the Radium Institute are preserved as the Curie Museum.

LYDIA MARIA ADAMS DEWITT

(b. 1859—d. 1928)

Lydia Maria Adams DeWitt was an American experimental pathologist and investigator of the chemotherapy of tuberculosis.

In 1878 she married Alton D. DeWitt, a teacher. Lydia DeWitt earned a medical degree at the University of Michigan in 1898 and taught anatomy there until 1908. She subsequently taught at Michigan State University (1908 – 10), Washington University (1910 – 12), and the University of Chicago (1912 – 26).

DeWitt is best known for her studies of the pathology of tuberculosis. She analyzed the linkages of dyes and toxic metals for the potential treatment of tuberculosis, and her investigations set the standard for later studies that led to the successful treatment of the disease. She also conducted influential investigations on the anatomy of the nervous system and on public health practices.

Her numerous publications include the coauthorship of the studies "Chemotherapy of Tuberculosis" (1893) and *The Chemistry of Tuberculosis* (1923).

GERTRUDE B. ELION

(b. 1918—d. 1999)

The U.S. pharmacologist Gertrude B. Elion received the Nobel Prize for Physiology or Medicine in 1988 along with George H. Hitchings and Sir James W. Black. The three were awarded the prize for their development of drugs used to treat several major diseases.

Gertrude Belle Elion was born on Jan. 23, 1918, in New York City. She graduated from Hunter College in New York City with a degree in biochemistry in 1937. Unable to obtain a graduate research position because she was a woman, she took a series of jobs, including lab assistant, chemistry and physics teacher in New York City high schools, and research chemist. During this time she also took classes at New York University, where she earned a master's degree in 1941. Because she could not devote herself to full-time studies, Elion never received a doctorate.

In 1944 Elion joined the Burroughs Wellcome Laboratories (now part of GlaxoSmithKline). There she was first the assistant and then the colleague of Hitchings, with whom she worked for the next four decades.

Gertrude B. Elion

Elion and Hitchings developed an array of new drugs that were effective against leukemia, autoimmune disorders, urinary-tract infections, gout, malaria, and viral herpes. Their success was due primarily to their innovative research methods. Rather than using the trial-and-error approach used by previous pharmacologists, Elion and Hitchings examined the difference between the biochemistry of normal human cells and that of cancer cells, bacteria, viruses, and other pathogens (disease-causing agents). They used this information to create drugs that could target a particular pathogen without harming the human host's normal cells. Their methods enabled them to eliminate much of the guesswork and wasted effort typical in previous drug research.

Although Elion officially retired in 1983, she helped oversee the development of azidothymidine (AZT), the first drug used in the treatment of AIDS. In 1991 she was awarded a National Medal of Science and was inducted into the National Women's Hall of Fame. She died on Feb. 21, 1999, in Chapel Hill, N.C.

ALICE EVANS

(b. 1881–d. 1975)

Alice Evans was an American scientist whose landmark work on pathogenic bacteria in dairy products was central in gaining acceptance of the pasteurization process to prevent disease.

After completing high school, Evans taught for four years before enrolling in a two-year course for rural teachers at Cornell University in Ithaca, New York. There she became interested in science and completed a B.S. at Cornell and an M.S. at the University of Wisconsin, Madison, both in bacteriology. She was encouraged to continue for a doctorate but chose instead to work on the bacteriology of milk and cheese for the dairy division of the U.S. Department of Agriculture. Her work on the bacteria of milk led to her groundbreaking work on brucellosis, a bacterial infection (not yet known by that name) that she determined could cause both spontaneous abortions in animals and remittent fever in humans.

Evans published the results of her work in 1918, but researchers, veterinarians, and physicians were skeptical of her claim that the pathogens were zoonotic (i.e., caused symptoms in animals and in humans). The dairy profession also scoffed at her warning that raw milk should be pasteurized to safeguard human health. Two years later, a scientist at the University of California proposed a new genus, Brucella, to include both the bacteria pathogenic to humans and those pathogenic to cattle, while Evans continued her work on various species of the bacteria. In 1922 Evans herself became infected, and for more than two decades she suffered periodic bouts of brucellosis.

Because of the pioneering work of Evans, by the late 1920s brucellosis was understood not only as an occupational hazard for farmers but also as a threat to the food supply. Once the American dairy industry reluctantly accepted the necessity of pasteurization of milk, the incidence of brucellosis declined. In recognition of her achievement, in 1928 the Society of American Bacteriologists elected Evans as the organization's first woman president. She retired in 1945, although she remained professionally active.

WILLIAMINA PATON STEVENS FLEMING

(b. 1857–d. 1911)

Williamina Paton Stevens Fleming was an American astronomer who pioneered in the classification of stellar spectra.

Mina Stevens was educated in public schools and from age 14 was a teacher as well as student. In May 1877 she married James O. Fleming, with whom she immigrated to the United States and settled in Boston the next year. The failure of her marriage in 1879 forced her to seek employment, and she soon became housekeeper for Edward C. Pickering, professor of astronomy and director of the Harvard College Observatory. Before the year was out Pickering had asked her to work at the observatory as a temporary employee, and in 1881 she became a permanent member of the research staff. For the next 30 years she collaborated on the analysis of stellar spectrum photography, and in 1898 she was appointed curator of astronomical photographs at Harvard.

Fleming is best known for her work on the classification of stellar spectra—the pattern of lines caused by the dispersion of a star's light through a prism placed before a telescope lens. Using a technique that came to be known as the Pickering-Fleming system, she studied the tens of thousands of celestial photographs taken for the Draper Memorial—a project dedicated to the amateur astronomer Henry Draper of New York. In the course of her work she discovered 10 novae, 52 nebulae, and hundreds of variable stars. She also established the first photographic standards of magnitude used to measure the variable brightness of stars.

Fleming's most important works include the *Draper Catalogue of Stellar Spectra* (1890), *A Photographic Study of Variable Stars* (1907), and *Stars Having Peculiar Spectra* (1912). In 1906 she became the first American woman elected to the Royal Astronomical Society. Her work provided the foundation for the future contributions of Annie Jump Cannon.

ALICE CUNNINGHAM FLETCHER
(b. 1838—d. 1923)

Alice Cunningham Fletcher was an American anthropologist whose stature as a social scientist, notably for her pioneer studies of Native American music, has overshadowed her influence on federal government Indian policies that later were considered to be unfortunate.

Fletcher taught school for a number of years, lectured occasionally on various topics, and was an early member and secretary of Sorosis and in 1873 a founder and secretary of the Association for the

Advancement of Women. A growing interest in archaeology and ethnology led to extensive reading in those fields, guided by Frederic Ward Putnam, director of Harvard's Peabody Museum, and by 1878 to fieldwork with American Indian remains in Florida and Massachusetts. In 1881 she went to Nebraska and began living among the Omaha. Her subsequent efforts to improve the lot of Native Americans reflected a missionary zeal and a paternalism toward Indians that was characteristic of the 19th century.

Concerned that the Omaha were about to be dispossessed, Fletcher went to Washington in 1882, drafted a bill to apportion Omaha tribal lands into individual Indian holdings, or allotments, and successfully lobbied for its passage in Congress. Appointed by President Chester A. Arthur to supervise the apportioning, she completed granting the land parcels in 1884 with the assistance of a young clerk in the Indian Bureau, Francis La Flesche, brother of writer-activist Susette La Flesche. The son of the principal Omaha chief, La Flesche lived with her as her adoptive son (unlegalized) and collaborated with her in her studies of native peoples and cultures.

Fletcher went to Alaska and the Aleutian Islands to study indigenous educational needs in 1886. Her tireless championing of Native American welfare—together with that of Mary Bonney and others—was instrumental in the passage of the Dawes General Allotment Act (1887), which further apportioned remaining tribal lands and provided for eventual citizenship for Native Americans. Though viewed as humanitarian at the time of its enactment, the Dawes Act came to be regarded as a public policy failure.

In the years following, Fletcher conducted land apportionment among the Winnebago and Nez Percé Indians and wrote *Indian Story and Song from North America* (1900) and *The Hako: A Pawnee Ceremony* (1904; reissued 1996). Her major work is thought to be *The Omaha Tribe* (1911), an exhaustive study written with Francis La Flesche. From 1899 to 1916 she was on the editorial board of the American Anthropologist, to which she was also a frequent contributor, and in 1908 she led in founding the School of American Archaeology (later the School of American Research) in Santa Fe, New Mexico.

DIAN FOSSEY

(b. 1932—d. 1985)

The U.S. zoologist Dian Fossey became the world's leading authority on the mountain gorilla. The data she gathered through years of observation greatly enlarged contemporary knowledge of the gorilla's habits, communication, and social structure.

Fossey was born on January 16, 1932, in San Francisco, California. She trained to become an occupational therapist at San Jose State College and graduated in 1954. She worked in that field for several years at a children's hospital in Louisville, Kentucky. In 1963 she took a trip to eastern Africa, where she met the anthropologist Louis Leakey and had her first glimpse of mountain gorillas. She returned to the United States after her trip, but in 1966 Leakey persuaded her to go back to Africa to study the mountain gorilla in its natural habitat on a long-term basis. To this end, she established the Karisoke Research Center in 1967 and began a hermitlike existence in Rwanda's Virunga Mountains, which was one of the last bastions of the endangered mountain gorilla. Through patient effort, Fossey was able to observe the animals and accustom them to her presence.

Fossey left Africa in 1970 to complete work for a doctorate at the University of Cambridge in England. In 1974 she received her degree in zoology with the completion of her dissertation, "The Behavior of the Mountain Gorilla." She returned to Rwanda with student volunteers who made broader kinds of research possible. Motivated by the killing of Digit, one of her favoured gorillas, Fossey generated international media coverage in 1978 in her battle against poachers.

In 1980 Fossey returned to the United States to accept a visiting associate professorship at Cornell University in Ithaca, New York. While teaching, Fossey also wrote *Gorillas in the Mist* (1983), which described her observations and argued for conservation of the gorillas; a film based on the book was released in 1988. Back in Rwanda, Fossey resumed her campaign against poachers, taking increasingly drastic measures to protect the Virunga gorillas. On December 26, 1985, her slain body was discovered near her campsite. Though no assailant was ever identified, it is widely suspected that she was killed by the poachers against whom she had struggled for so long.

ROSALIND FRANKLIN
(b. 1920—d. 1958)

A British biophysicist, Rosalind Franklin is best known for her contributions to the discovery of the molecular structure of deoxyribonucleic acid (DNA). DNA is the chief substance composing chromosomes and genes, the hereditary material. When Francis Crick, James Watson, and Maurice Wilkins were awarded the 1962 Nobel Prize for Physiology or medicine for determining the structure of the DNA molecule, many scientists believed that Franklin should have been honored with them.

Born in London on July 25, 1920, Rosalind Elsie Franklin won a scholarship to Newnham College, Cambridge. After graduation in 1941 she began research on the physical structure of coals and carbonized coals. Working in Paris from 1947 to 1950, she gained skill in using X-ray diffraction as an analytical technique. (X-ray diffraction is a method of analyzing the crystal structure of materials by passing X-rays through them and observing the diffraction, or scattering, image of the rays.) Franklin used this technique to describe the structure of carbons with more precision than had previously been possible. She also determined that there are two distinct classes of carbons—those that form graphite when they are heated to high temperatures and those that do not.

In 1951 Franklin joined the King's College Medical Research Council biophysics unit. With Raymond Gosling she conducted X-ray diffraction studies of the molecular structure of DNA. Based on these studies, she at first concluded that the structure was helical (having spiral arms). Later research caused her to change her mind, and it was left to Watson and Crick to develop the double-helix model of the molecule that proved to be consistent with DNA's known properties. Some of the data used by those scientists in their successful effort, however, was first produced by Franklin.

From 1953 until her death on April 16, 1958, Franklin worked at the crystallography laboratory of Birkbeck College, London. There she published her earlier work on coals and helped determine the structure of the tobacco mosaic virus.

SOPHIE GERMAIN

(b. 1776—d. 1831)

Marie-Sophie Germain was a French mathematician who contributed notably to the study of acoustics, elasticity, and the theory of numbers.

As a girl Germain read widely in her father's library and then later, using the pseudonym of M. Le Blanc, managed to obtain lecture notes for courses from the newly organized École Polytechnique in Paris. It was through the École Polytechnique that she met the mathematician Joseph-Louis Lagrange, who remained a strong source of support and encouragement to her for several years. Germain's early work was in number theory, her interest having been stimulated by Adrien-Marie Legendre's *Théorie des nombres* (1789) and by Carl Friedrich Gauss's *Disquisitiones Arithmeticae* (1801). This subject occupied her throughout her life and eventually provided her most significant result. In 1804 she initiated a correspondence with Gauss under her male pseudonym. Gauss only learned of her true identity when Germain, fearing for Gauss's safety as a result of the French occupation of Hannover in 1807, asked a family friend in the French army to ascertain his whereabouts and ensure that he would not be ill-treated.

In 1809 the French Academy of Sciences offered a prize for a mathematical account of the phenomena exhibited in experiments on vibrating plates conducted by the German physicist Ernst F.F. Chladni. In 1811 Germain submitted an anonymous memoir, but the prize was not awarded. The competition was reopened twice more, once in 1813 and again in 1816, and Germain submitted a memoir on each occasion. Her third memoir, with which she finally won the prize, treated vibrations of general curved as well as plane surfaces and was published privately in 1821. During the 1820s she worked on generalizations of her research but, isolated from the academic community on account of her gender and thus largely unaware of new developments taking place in the theory of elasticity, she made little real progress. In 1816 Germain met Joseph Fourier, whose friendship and position in the Academy helped her to participate more fully in Parisian scientific life, but his reservations about her work on elasticity eventually led him to distance himself from her professionally, although they remained close friends.

Meanwhile Germain had actively revived her interest in number theory and in 1819 wrote to Gauss outlining her strategy for a general solution to Fermat's last theorem. Her result first appeared in 1825 in a supplement to the second edition of Legendre's *Théorie des nombres*. She corresponded extensively with Legendre, and her method formed the basis for his proof of the theorem for the case n = 5. The theorem was proved for all cases by the English mathematician Andrew Wiles in 1995.

LILLIAN EVELYN GILBRETH

(b. 1878—d. 1972)

Lillian Evelyn Gilbreth, née Lillian Evelyn Moller, was an American psychologist and engineer who, with her husband, Frank Bunker Gilbreth, developed methods to increase the efficiency of industrial employees, most notably time-and-motion study.

Moller received bachelor's and master's degrees in literature from the University of California, Berkeley, and had begun her doctoral studies when she married Frank Gilbreth in 1904. She quickly adopted her husband's enthusiasm for workplace efficiency, and the two collaborated on applying the social sciences to industrial management, emphasizing the worker rather than nonhuman factors. Their method of time-and-motion study provided a systematic means of identifying and analyzing the number of movements and the amount of time needed to complete a specific task. *Motion Study* (1911) was the first important publication of their research. Lillian switched the focus of her graduate study from literature to psychology and earned a doctorate from Brown University in 1915. Her psychological expertise complemented Frank's physiological and mechanical insights in their later writings *Fatigue Study* (1916) and *Applied Motion Study* (1917).

After her husband's death in 1924, Gilbreth assumed the presidency of his consulting firm and remained active in research, lecturing, and writing. She held teaching positions at Purdue University (1935—48), the Newark College of Engineering (1941—43), and the University of Wisconsin (1955). Two of the Gilbreths' 12 children—Frank Bunker Gilbreth, Jr., and Ernestine Gilbreth Carey—humorously described their parents' domestic application of efficiency programs in the popular books *Cheaper by the Dozen* (1949; filmed 1950, 2003) and *Belles on Their Toes* (1950; filmed 1952).

JANE GOODALL
(b. 1934)

British ethologist Jane Goodall is best known for her exceptionally detailed and long-term research on the chimpanzees of Gombe Stream National Park in Tanzania. Over the years she was able to correct a number of misunderstandings about these animals.

Goodall was born on April 3, 1934, in London, England. She was interested in animal behavior from an early age. After leaving school when she was 18 years old, she worked as a secretary and as a film production assistant until she gained passage to Africa. Once there, Goodall began assisting paleontologist and anthropologist Louis Leakey. Her association with Leakey led eventually to her establishment in June 1960 of a camp in the Gombe Stream Game Reserve (now a national park) so that she could observe the behavior of chimpanzees in the region.

In 1964 Goodall married a Dutch photographer who had been sent in 1962 to Tanzania to film her work (they later divorced). The University of Cambridge awarded Goodall a Ph.D. in ethology in 1965; she was one of very few candidates to receive a doctoral degree without having first possessed a bachelor's degree. Except for short periods of absence, Goodall and her family remained in Gombe until 1975, often directing the

Jane Goodall

fieldwork of other doctoral candidates. In 1977 she cofounded the Jane Goodall Institute for Wildlife Research, Education, and Conservation in California. The center later moved its headquarters to Washington, D.C.

During her research, Goodall found that chimpanzees are omnivorous, not vegetarian, and that they are capable of making and using tools. She also discovered that they have a set of complex and highly developed social behaviors that were previously unrecognized by humans.

Goodall wrote a number of books and articles about various aspects of her work, notably *In the Shadow of Man* (1971). She summarized her years of observation in *The Chimpanzees of Gombe: Patterns of Behavior* (1986). Goodall continued to write and lecture about environmental and conservation issues into the early 21st century. The recipient of numerous honors, she was created Dame of the British Empire in 2003.

TEMPLE GRANDIN

(b. 1947)

U.S. scientist and industrial designer Temple Grandin created systems to counter stress in certain human and animal populations. Her professional work grew from her own experience with autism.

Grandin was born on August 29, 1947, in Boston, Massachusetts. At the age of three she was unable to talk, and she exhibited many behavioral problems. Doctors diagnosed her as autistic and suggested to her family that they place her in an institution. Instead, however, her parents sent her to a series of private schools, where her high IQ was nurtured. She graduated in 1970 from Franklin Pierce College in New Hampshire, where she majored in experimental psychology. Next she earned a master's degree at Arizona State University in Tempe and a doctorate at the

Temple Grandin

University of Illinois at Urbana-Champaign, both in animal science. In 1990 she began teaching that subject at Colorado State University in Fort Collins, where she also ran Grandin Livestock Systems.

Aware that intense fear, born of a hypersensitivity to sound and touch, is common both to autistic people and to animals, Grandin devoted her life to devising systems to alleviate the anxiety of both groups. While still in high school she designed a "squeeze machine" to relieve her own nervous tension, modeling it on a chute fashioned to hold animals in place during branding and other procedures. Improved versions of her machine are widely used not only in schools for autistic children but also by autistic adults. The main focus of Grandin's career was the design of humane livestock facilities that eliminate pain and fear from the slaughtering process. Her designs enable workers to move animals without frightening them.

Grandin wrote or edited several books on the humane treatment of animals. She also spoke widely about her experiences with autism. A television movie about her life, *Temple Grandin*, was released in 2010.

EVELYN GRANVILLE

(b. 1924)

Evelyn Granville, née Evelyn Boyd, is an American mathematician who was one of the first African American women to receive a doctoral degree in mathematics.

Boyd received an undergraduate degree in mathematics and physics from Smith College, Northampton, Mass., in 1945. She received a doctoral degree in mathematics in 1949 from Yale University, New Haven, Conn., where she studied under Einar Hille. She was the second African American woman to receive a doctorate in mathematics. From 1949 to 1950 she had a postdoctoral fellowship at New York University, and from 1950 to 1952 she was an associate professor of mathematics at Fisk University, Nashville, Tenn.

In 1952 Boyd became a mathematician at the National Bureau of Standards (NBS) in Washington, D.C., where she worked on missile fuses. Her division of NBS was later absorbed by the United States Army and became the Diamond Ordnance Fuze Laboratories. There she became interested in the new field of computer programming, which led her to the corporation International Business Machines (IBM) in 1956. She worked on programs in the assembly language SOAP and later in FORTRAN for the IBM 650, which was the first computer intended for use in businesses, and the IBM 704. In 1957 she joined IBM's Vanguard Computing Center in Washington, D.C., where she wrote computer programs that tracked orbits for the unmanned Vanguard satellite and the manned Mercury spacecraft. She left IBM in 1960 to move to Los Angeles, where she worked at the aerospace firm Space Technology Laboratories; there she did further work on satellite orbits. In 1962 she joined the aerospace firm North American Aviation, where she worked on celestial mechanics and trajectory calculations for the Apollo project. She returned to IBM to its Federal Systems Division in 1963 as senior mathematician.

Boyd returned to academic life in 1967 as an assistant professor of mathematics at California State University, Los Angeles. Teaching the mathematics course that was required for those who wished to become elementary school teachers led to an interest in mathematics education. She married Edward Granville in 1970. In 1975 she and her colleague Jason Frand wrote a textbook, *Theory and Applications of Mathematics for Teachers*. From 1985 to 1988 she taught computer science and mathematics at Texas College in Tyler, and in 1990 she was appointed professor of mathematics at the University of Texas, also in Tyler. She retired in 1997.

CLAUDIE HAIGNERÉ

(b. 1957)

Claudie Haigneré is a French cosmonaut, doctor, and politician, and the first French woman in space.

Haigneré graduated as a rheumatologist from Faculté de Médecine and Faculté des Sciences in Paris and completed a doctorate in neurosciences in 1992. From 1984 to 1992 she worked at the

Cochin Hospital in Paris in rheumatology and rehabilitation. In 1985 she was selected as a candidate astronaut by the French space agency, Centre National d'Etudes Spatiales (CNES). After her selection she conducted research on the effect of space travel on human physiology, specifically the adaptation of cognitive and motor skills in a microgravity environment. In 1992 she was named the alternate to French cosmonaut Jean-Pierre Haigneré (whom she married in 2001) for "Altair," the Franco-Russian Soyuz TM-17 space mission, which launched in July 1993. In 1994 Haigneré was selected for the Franco-Russian "Cassiope" mission and began training at the Yury Gagarin Cosmonaut Training Centre in Star City, Russia. On Aug. 17, 1996, she launched into space aboard Soyuz TM-24 with two Russian cosmonauts, commander Valery Korzun and flight engineer Aleksandr Kaleri, and docked with the Mir space station. She returned to Earth on Sept. 2, 1996, on Soyuz TM-23.

Claudie Haigneré

In 1999 she became the first woman qualified to command a Soyuz capsule during reentry. On Oct. 21, 2001, she became the first female European cosmonaut to take part in a flight to the International Space Station (ISS) when she served as flight engineer on Soyuz TM-33 with two Russian cosmonauts, commander Viktor Afanasiyev and flight engineer Konstantin Kozeyev. After nearly 10 days in space, her crew flew Soyuz TM-32 back to Earth on October 31, leaving the newer Soyuz TM-33 as an emergency craft for the ISS crew.

From 2002 to 2005 Haigneré served in several political positions in France, including minister for research and new technologies, minister for European affairs, and secretary-general for Franco-German cooperation. In November 2005 the European Space Agency chose her to be adviser to the director general.

ALICE HAMILTON

(b. 1869—d. 1970)

Alice Hamilton was an American pathologist, known for her research on industrial diseases.

Hamilton received her medical degree from the University of Michigan (1893) and continued her studies at Johns Hopkins University and in Germany. From 1897 to 1919 she was a resident of Hull House in Chicago. She became the first female faculty member at Harvard Medical School (1919—35) and did studies for the state of Illinois, the federal government, and the League of Nations. By actively publicizing the danger to workers' health of industrial toxic substances such as lead and mercury, she contributed to the passage of workers' compensation laws and to the development of safer working conditions. Her writings include *Industrial Toxicology* (1934; 4th ed., 1983) and an autobiography, *Exploring the Dangerous Trades* (1943).

ANNA JANE HARRISON

(b. 1912—d. 1998)

Anna Jane Harrison, also known as Anna J. Harrison, was an American chemist and educator who in 1978 became the first woman president of the American Chemical Society. She was known for her advocacy for increased public awareness of science.

Harrison grew up on a farm in rural Missouri. Her father died when she was seven, leaving her mother to manage the family farm and to care for Harrison and her elder brother. Harrison's formative education took place in a one-room schoolhouse near her home. She later attended high school in a nearby town. Harrison's intellectual interests eventually led her to the University of Missouri, where she earned a bachelor's degree in 1933. She then returned to her hometown to teach at the same rural one-room school she had attended in her youth. Two years later, however, she resumed studies at the university, this time as a graduate student in physical chemistry. After receiving a master's degree in 1937, she published a paper on photovoltaic effects (voltages generated by interactions between dissimilar chemicals when struck by light) in solutions of Grignard reagents (organic derivatives of magnesium). She also began work toward a doctorate, which she earned in 1940. Her dissertation research focused on the association of sodium ketyls (a type of radical).

Upon completing her doctorate studies, Harrison took a post as an instructor of chemistry at H. Sophie Newcomb Memorial College, a women's college at Tulane University in New Orleans. Over the course of the next several years, she also performed research for the National Defense Research Council and for Corning Glass Works and continued to study ketyl association. In 1945 she joined the faculty at Mount Holyoke College, a women's school in South Hadley, Mass., where she was elevated to full professor in 1950 and was chair of the department of chemistry from 1960 to 1966. At Mount Holyoke, Harrison contributed to research on ultraviolet light and photolysis, or the breakdown of molecules via light absorption.

In the 1970s Harrison became increasingly outspoken about the need for improving the communication of science to the public and in particular to public officials. Following her election as president of the American Chemical Society, she continued to champion the importance of cultivating a scientifically informed public. She encouraged her colleagues to view the chemical profession as fundamental to not only the advancement of scientific knowledge but also the improvement of science education, public awareness of science, and public welfare.

In 1979 Harrison retired from Mount Holyoke. However, she remained active in promoting the communication of science and served on multiple scientific councils. From 1983 to 1984 she was president of the American Association for the Advancement of Science (AAAS), and in 1989, with former Mount Holyoke colleague Edwin S. Weaver, she published *Chemistry: A Search to Understand*. The authors described the work as suited for students who were "intellectually curious but not professionally driven" in the field of chemistry. Harrison received many honours throughout her career and was celebrated for having inspired numerous young women to pursue careers in science.

SUSAN HELMS

(b. 1958)

Susan Helms, in full Susan Jane Helms, is a U.S. astronaut and Air Force officer who was the first U.S. military woman in space and, with astronaut James Voss, performed the longest space walk.

Helms received a bachelor's degree in aeronautical engineering from the U.S. Air Force Academy in Colorado Springs, Colo., in 1980 and was commissioned as a second lieutenant. From 1980 to 1984 she worked as a weapons separation engineer on the F-15 and F-16 aircraft at Eglin Air Force Base, Fla. She received a master's degree in aeronautics and astronautics from Stanford University in Stanford, Calif., in 1985 and was an assistant professor of aeronautics at the Air Force Academy from 1985 to 1987. She graduated from the U.S. Air Force Test Pilot School at Edwards Air Force Base, Calif., in 1988, and as an exchange officer, she was a test engineer on the CF-18 at the Canadian Forces Base at Cold Lake, Alta., from 1989 to 1990. She was selected by the National Aeronautics and Space Administration (NASA) as an astronaut in 1990.

Helms made five spaceflights, the first on the STS-54 mission (Jan. 13—19, 1993) of the space shuttle *Endeavour*, which launched a Tracking and Data Relay Satellite. Her second spaceflight, STS-64 (Sept. 9—20, 1994) on *Discovery*, carried an experiment that used lasers to measure aerosols in Earth's atmosphere. The STS-78 mission of the space shuttle *Columbia* carried a pressurized Spacelab module in which the crew performed biological and materials science experiments. Helms was the payload commander of the Spacelab module. The mission lasted nearly 17 days (June 20—July 7, 1996) and at the time was the longest space shuttle flight.

On Helms's fourth spaceflight, STS-101 (May 19—29, 2000) on the space shuttle *Atlantis*, the crew made repairs to the International Space

Susan Helms

Station (ISS) to prepare it for its first crew. She returned to the ISS on the space shuttle *Discovery*'s STS-102 mission (launched March 8, 2001). Helms, astronaut James Voss, and cosmonaut Yury Usachyov were the ISS's second resident crew. (Helms, Voss, and Usachyov had also flown together on STS-101.) On March 11 Helms and Voss performed a space walk that made room for a temporary storage module and that lasted 8 hours 56 minutes, making it the longest space walk ever. On July 15 Helms used the ISS's robotic arm to remove the Quest air lock from the payload bay of the space shuttle *Atlantis* and attach it to the ISS. Helms returned to Earth on Aug. 22, 2001, on the space shuttle *Discovery*'s STS-105 mission. On her five flights, she had spent a total of nearly 211 days in space.

Helms left NASA in 2002 to return to the Air Force, where she was named chief of the space superiority division of the Space Command in Colorado Springs. From 2004 to 2005 she was vice commander of the 45th Space Wing at Patrick Air Force Base, Fla. The next year she became a deputy director at the Air Education and Training Command at Randolph Air Force Base, Tex. In 2006 she returned to the 45th Space Wing as commander. In 2008 she became director of plans and policy at the U.S. Strategic Command at Offutt Air Force Base, Neb., and in 2009 she reached the rank of major general. In 2011 she was promoted to lieutenant general and became commander of both the 14th Air Force of the Air Force Space Command and the Joint Functional Component Command for Space at Vandenberg Air Force Base, Calif.

CAROLINE LUCRETIA HERSCHEL
(b. 1750—d. 1848)

Caroline Lucretia Herschel was a German-born British astronomer noted for her contributions to the astronomical researches of her brother, Sir William Herschel; she executed many of the calculations connected with his studies and, on her own, detected by telescope three nebulae in 1783 and eight comets from 1786 to 1797.

Caroline assisted her mother in the management of the household until 1772, when her brother, William, took her to Bath, Eng., where he had established himself as a teacher of music. Once settled in Bath, Caroline trained and performed successfully as a singer. Both she and William gave their last public musical performance in 1782, when her brother accepted the private office of court astronomer to George III. In addition to keeping house for her brother and grinding and polishing mirrors, she began executing the laborious calculations that were connected with his observations. As her interest grew, she swept the heavens with a small Newtonian reflector and made her own observations and astronomical discoveries. In 1787 the king gave her an annual pension of £50 in her capacity as her brother's assistant. In 1798 she presented to the Royal Society an Index to Flamsteed's observations, together with a catalog of 560 stars omitted from the *British Catalogue* and a list of the errata in that publication.

She returned to Hannover after William's death in 1822 and soon completed the cataloging of 2,500 nebulae and many star clusters. In 1828 (when she was 77) the Astronomical Society awarded her its gold medal for an unpublished revision and reorganization of their work. She lived some 20 years longer and continued to receive the respect and admiration of both scientists and the general public.

DOROTHY CROWFOOT HODGKIN

(b. 1910—d. 1994)

The English chemist Dorothy Crowfoot Hodgkin was awarded the Nobel Prize for Chemistry in 1964 for her work in determining the structure of vitamin B12. In 1948 she and her colleagues made the first X-ray diffraction photograph of the vitamin. Until then normal chemical methods had revealed little of the structure of the central part of the molecule, at the heart of which is a cobalt atom. The atomic arrangement of the compound was eventually determined through the techniques that Hodgkin helped develop.

Dorothy Mary Crowfoot was born on May 12, 1910, in Cairo, Egypt. She studied in England at the Sir John Leman School and at Somerville College, Oxford. While at Oxford she studied X rays of complicated macromolecules. In 1934 she and a colleague at Cambridge University made the first X-ray diffraction photograph of the protein pepsin. She returned to Somerville College later in 1934 as a tutor in chemistry. In 1937 she married Thomas Hodgkin, a lecturer and writer. From 1942 to 1949 she worked on a structural analysis of penicillin.

Hodgkin became a fellow of the Royal Society in 1947, professor of the Royal Society at Oxford University (1960–77), and a member of the Order of Merit in 1965. She spent the early 1960s in Africa at the University of Ghana, where her husband directed the Institute of African Studies. She was appointed chancellor of Bristol University in 1970 and an honorary fellow there in 1988. She was also a fellow of Wolfson College, Oxford (1977–83). Hodgkin died on July 29, 1994, in Shipston-on-Stour, Warwickshire, England.

GRACE HOPPER

(b. 1906—d. 1992)

After graduating from Vassar College (B.A., 1928), Grace Hopper attended Yale University (M.A., 1930; Ph.D., 1934). She taught mathematics at Vassar before joining the Naval Reserve in 1943. She became a lieutenant and was assigned to the Bureau of Ordnance's Computation Project at Harvard University (1944), where she worked on Mark I, the first large-scale automatic calculator and a precursor of electronic computers. She remained at Harvard as a civilian research fellow while maintaining her naval career as a reservist. After a moth infiltrated the circuits of Mark I, she coined the term bug to refer to unexplained computer failures.

In 1949 Hopper joined the Eckert-Mauchly Computer Corp., where she designed an improved compiler, which translated a programmer's instructions into computer codes. She remained with the firm when it was taken over by Remington Rand (1951) and by Sperry Rand Corp. (1955). In 1957 her division developed Flow-Matic, the first English-language data-processing compiler. She retired from the navy with the rank of commander in 1966, but she was recalled to active duty the following year to help standardize the navy's computer languages. At the age of 79, she was the oldest officer on active U.S. naval duty when she retired again in 1986.

Hopper was elected a fellow of the Institute of Electrical and Electronic Engineers (1962), was named the first computer science Man of the Year by the Data Processing Management Association (1969), and was awarded the National Medal of Technology (1991).

LIBBIE HENRIETTA HYMAN

(b. 1888—d. 1969)

Libbie Henrietta Hyman was a U.S. zoologist and writer particularly noted for her widely used texts and reference works on invertebrate and vertebrate zoology.

Hyman received her Ph.D. degree from the University of Chicago (1915), where she had a research appointment (1916–31) under the distinguished zoologist Charles Manning Child. Much of her work during that period was on flatworms. She held an honorary research appointment (1937–69) to the American Museum of Natural History in New York City until her death.

Among her important works were *A Laboratory Manual for Elementary Zoology* (1919), *A Laboratory Manual for Comparative Vertebrate Zoology* (1922), *Comparative Vertebrate Anatomy* (1942), and *The Invertebrates, 6 vol.*, (1940–68), a monumental work still incomplete at the time of her death. She served as editor of *Systematic Zoology* (1959–63) and as president of the Society of Systematic Zoology (1959).

HYPATIA

(355 CE?—415)

The ancient Egyptian scholar Hypatia lived in Alexandria, Egypt, during the final years of the Roman Empire. She was the world's leading mathematician and astronomer of the time. She was also an important teacher of philosophy.

The year of Hypatia's birth is uncertain; she may have been born about 355. She was the daughter of Theon of Alexandria, a leading mathematician and astronomer who belonged to the Alexandrian Museum, a famous center of learning. Theon taught Hypatia mathematics, science, literature, philosophy, and art.

Theon edited an important edition of Euclid's *Elements*, and he wrote commentaries on works by Ptolemy. Hypatia continued her father's program, which was essentially an effort to preserve the Greek mathematical and astronomical heritage during extremely difficult times. She wrote commentaries on works of geometry, number theory (an advanced branch of arithmetic), and astronomy. Unfortunately, none of her works has survived. Hypatia was also a popular teacher and lecturer on philosophy, attracting many loyal students and large audiences. She rose to become head of Alexandria's Neoplatonist school of philosophy, a school whose basic ideas derived from Plato.

Hypatia lived during a difficult time in Alexandria's history. The city was embroiled in a bitter religious conflict between Christians, Jews, and pagans (who believed in many gods). In 391 the Christian bishop of Alexandria had a pagan temple destroyed, even though it contained an important collection of classical literature that could not be replaced. Although Hypatia's teachings were not religious, some Christians saw them as pagan. Her views became less accepted in the city. In March 415 Hypatia was brutally murdered by a mob of Christian extremists. She became a powerful symbol of female learning and science and of scholarly pursuits in the face of ignorant prejudice.

LISA JACKSON

(b. 1962)

U.S. public official Lisa Jackson served as commissioner of New Jersey's department of environmental protection from 2006 to 2008. In 2009 she became administrator of the Environmental Protection Agency (EPA) under President Barack Obama's administration.

Lisa Perez Jackson was born on Feb. 8, 1962, in Philadelphia, Pa., but grew up in New Orleans. She studied chemical engineering, graduating from Tulane University with a bachelor's degree in 1983 and from Princeton University with a master's degree in 1986. She took a job with the EPA the following year. While there, Jackson was responsible for the cleanup of industrial sites under the federal Superfund program, and she managed enforcement programs in New York and New Jersey.

In 2002 Jackson became director of the enforcement division for New Jersey's department of environmental protection. She transitioned to the office of land use manage-

Lisa Jackson

ment and then was promoted to commissioner of the department of environmental protection in 2006. During her term, she increased enforcement efforts, pledged to reduce carbon emissions in the state, and placed a moratorium on the hunting of black bears. She was named chief of staff to New Jersey Governor Jon Corzine in October 2008, and she assumed the duties of that office on December 1. Two weeks later, however, President-elect Obama nominated her to head the EPA. When the Senate confirmed her appointment in January 2009, Jackson became the first African American to hold the post.

MAE JEMISON

(b. 1956)

Trained as a physician and engineer, Mae Jemison was the first African American woman to become an astronaut. In 1992 she spent eight days orbiting Earth as a science mission specialist aboard the space shuttle *Endeavour*.

Mae Carol Jemison was born on October 17, 1956, in Decatur, Alabama, the youngest of three children. Her father was a maintenance worker, and her mother was a schoolteacher. When Jemison was three years old, the family moved to Chicago, Illinois. The Jemisons encouraged their youngest daughter's wide-ranging interests, which included anthropology, archaeology, evolution, and astronomy, as well as dance. Jemison graduated from high school at the age of 16 and entered Stanford University in California, where in 1977 she received undergraduate degrees in chemical engineering and African American studies. Later in the same year she began studying medicine at Cornell University in New York. She was particularly interested in international medicine and volunteered to work for a summer in a Cambodian refugee camp in Thailand. In 1979 she studied in Kenya. After graduating from medical school in 1981, she worked briefly as a general practitioner in Los Angeles, California, before joining the U.S. Peace Corps. From 1983 to 1985 she served as a Peace Corps medical officer in the African countries of Sierra Leone and Liberia, providing medical care for Peace Corps and U.S. embassy personnel. While in Africa, she also conducted research for the National Institutes of Health and the Centers for Disease Control.

When she returned to the United States in 1985, Jemison resumed work as a general practitioner. She also studied engineering in preparation for her application to the astronaut training program of the National Aeronautics and Space Administration (NASA). In October 1986 she learned that, of 2,000 applicants, she was one of 15 selected for the astronaut training program. After completing her training as a space shuttle mission specialist in 1988, she began working as a member of the support team for shuttle missions at the Kennedy Space Center at Cape Canaveral, Florida. In September 1992 Jemison served as a mission specialist on the space shuttle *Endeavour* for the STS-47 Spacelab J mission. She conducted experiments on the effect of weightlessness on human and animal biology. At the time of her flight, she was the only African American female astronaut.

Jemison left NASA in March 1993 to start her own company, the Jemison Group. The company develops advanced technologies in the areas of health care, food production, and environmental protection that are specifically targeted for use in developing countries. BioSentient

Mae Jemison aboard the space shuttle *Endeavour*

Corporation, a company Jemison founded in 1999, develops health-monitoring equipment that patients can wear on their bodies. From 1995 to 2002 Jemison taught environmental studies at Dartmouth College. She is the recipient of numerous awards and honorary degrees. Her book, *Find Where the Wind Goes: Moments from My Life* (2001), provides an autobiographical account of her childhood and youth.

IRÈNE JOLIOT-CURIE
(b. 1897—d. 1956)

French physicist and chemist Irène Joliot-Curie received the 1935 Nobel Prize for Chemistry jointly with her husband, Frédéric Joliot-Curie. She was born in Paris on Sept. 12, 1897, the daughter of the Nobel Prize–winning scientists Pierre and Marie Curie. She worked as a researcher in the Curie Laboratory from 1921 to 1935 and then at the Institut du Radium of the University of Paris from 1937 to 1956. She served as undersecretary of scientific research in the French cabinet in 1936. The Joliot-Curies were awarded the Nobel prize for synthesizing new radioactive elements. They also demonstrated the splitting of uranium. Irène Joliot-Curie died on March 17, 1956, in Paris.

ADA KING, COUNTESS OF LOVELACE
(b. 1815—d. 1852)

Ada King, countess of Lovelace, was an English mathematician and an associate of Charles Babbage, for whose prototype of a digital computer she created a program. She has been called the first computer programmer.

She was the daughter of famed poet Lord Byron and Annabella

Milbanke Byron, who legally separated two months after her birth. Her father then left Britain forever, and his daughter never knew him personally. She was educated privately by tutors and then self-educated but was helped in her advanced studies by mathematician-logician Augustus De Morgan, the first professor of mathematics at the University of London. On July 8, 1835, she married William King, 8th Baron King; and, when he was created an earl in 1838, she became countess of Lovelace.

She became interested in Babbage's machines as early as 1833 and, most notably, in 1843 came to translate and annotate an article written by the Italian mathematician and engineer Luigi Federico Menabrea, *Notions sur la machine analytique de Charles Babbage* (1842; *Elements of Charles Babbage's Analytical Machine*). Her detailed and elaborate annotations (especially her description of how the proposed Analytical Engine could be programmed to compute Bernoulli numbers) were excellent; "the Analytical Engine," she said, "weaves algebraic patterns, just as the Jacquard-loom weaves flowers and leaves."

YELENA KONDAKOVA

(b. 1957)

Yelena Kondakova is a Russian cosmonaut who was the first woman to make a long-duration spaceflight.

Kondakova graduated from the Bauman Moscow Higher Technical School in 1980 and then worked for the aerospace manufacturer Energia as an engineer. In 1985 she married cosmonaut Valery Ryumin. She was selected for the cosmonaut program in 1989.

On Oct. 4, 1994, Kondakova made her first spaceflight, as flight engineer on board Soyuz TM-20, which flew to the Russian space station Mir. She spent about 169 days in space, during which she and her crewmates had to contend with power failures and mechanical problems aboard the aging space station. It was during this flight that the American space shuttle first rendezvoused with Mir; however, no docking was made.

Yelena Kondakova

On her second spaceflight Kondakova was a mission specialist on the STS-84 mission on board the American space shuttle *Atlantis*, which launched on May 15, 1997. Kondakova and the crew of *Atlantis* transferred equipment and supplies to Mir. *Atlantis* landed on May 24 after having spent nine days in space.

In 1999 Kondakova left the cosmonaut program and was elected to the Russian legislative body the Duma as a deputy for the Fatherland—All Russia party (after 2001, the United Russia party).

Sofya Vasilyevna Kovalevskaya

(b. 1850—d. 1891)

Sofya Vasilyevna Kovalevskaya was a mathematician and writer who made a valuable contribution to the theory of partial differential equations. She was the first woman in modern Europe to gain a doctorate in mathematics, the first to join the editorial board of a scientific journal, and the first to be appointed professor of mathematics.

In 1868 Kovalevskaya entered into a marriage of convenience with a young paleontologist, Vladimir Kovalevsky, in order to leave Russia and continue her studies. The pair traveled together to Austria and then to Germany, where in 1869 she studied at the University of Heidelberg under the mathematicians Leo Königsberger and Paul du Bois-Reymond and the physicist Hermann von Helmholtz. The following year she moved to Berlin, where, having been refused admission to the university on account of her gender, she studied privately with the mathematician Karl Weierstrass. In 1874 she presented three papers—on partial differential equations, on Saturn's rings, and on elliptic integrals—to the University of Göttingen as her doctoral dissertation and was awarded the degree, summa cum laude, in absentia. Her paper on partial differential equations, the most important of the three papers, won her valuable recognition within the European mathematical community. It contains what is now commonly known as the Cauchy-Kovalevskaya theorem, which gives conditions for the existence of solutions to a certain class of partial differential equations. Having gained her degree, she returned to Russia, where her daughter was born in 1878. She separated permanently from her husband in 1881.

In 1883 Kovalevskaya accepted Magnus Mittag-Leffler's invitation to become a lecturer in mathematics at the University of Stockholm. She was promoted to full professor in 1889. In 1884 she joined the editorial board of the mathematical journal *Acta Mathematica*, and in 1888 she became the first woman to be elected a corresponding member of the Russian Academy of Sciences. In 1888 she was awarded the Prix Bordin of the French Academy of Sciences for a paper on the rotation of a solid body around a fixed point.

Kovalevskaya also gained a reputation as a writer, an advocate of women's rights, and a champion of radical political causes. She composed novels, plays, and essays, including the autobiographical *Memories of Childhood* (1890) and *The Nihilist Woman* (1892), a depiction of her life in Russia.

HEDY LAMARR
(b. 1913/14—d. 2000)

Hedy Lamarr was a glamorous Austrian film star who was often typecast as a provocative femme fatale. Years after her screen career ended, she achieved recognition as a noted inventor of a radio communications device.

The daughter of a prosperous Viennese banker, Lamarr was privately tutored from age four; by the time she was 10, she was a proficient pianist and dancer and could speak four languages. At age 16 she enrolled in Max Reinhardt's Berlin-based dramatic school, and within a year she made her motion picture debut in *Geld Auf der Strasse* (1930; *Money on the Street*). She achieved both stardom and notoriety in the Czech film *Extase* (1932; Ecstasy), in which she briefly but tastefully appeared in the nude. Her burgeoning career was halted by her 1933 marriage to Austrian munitions manufacturer Fritz Mandl, who not only prohibited her from further stage and screen appearances but also tried unsuccessfully to destroy all existing prints of *Extase*. After leaving the possessive Mandl, she went to Hollywood in 1937, where she appeared in her first English-language film, the classic romantic drama *Algiers* (1938).

Under contract to Metro-Goldwyn-Mayer from 1938 to 1945, she displayed her acting skills in such films as *H.M. Pulham, Esq.* (1941) and *Tortilla Flat* (1942). For the most part, however, she was confined to mostly decorative roles, such as that of *Tondelayo in White Cargo* (1942).

Hedy Lamarr

Hoping to secure more substantial parts, she set up her own production company in 1946, but within three years she returned to her exotic stock-in-trade in Cecil B. DeMille's *Samson and Delilah* (1949), her most commercially successful film.

Lamarr once insisted, "Any girl can be glamorous; all you have to do is stand still and look stupid." That she herself was anything but stupid was unequivocally proved during World War II when, in collaboration with the avant-garde composer George Antheil, she invented an electronic device that minimized the jamming of radio signals. Though it was never used in wartime, this device is a component of present-day satellite and cellular phone technology.

Retiring from movies in 1958 (except for a cameo appearance in *Instant Karma*, 1990), Lamarr subsequently resurfaced in 1966 and 1991 when she was arrested on, and later cleared of, shoplifting charges; when she sued the collaborators on her 1966 autobiography *Ecstasy and Me* for misrepresentation; and when she took director Mel Brooks to court for including a character named Hedley Lamarr in his western spoof *Blazing Saddles* (1974). She was married six times (her husbands included screenwriter Gene Markey and actor John Loder) but was living alone at the time of her death.

MARY DOUGLAS LEAKEY

(b. 1913—d. 1996)

Mary Douglas Leakey was an English-born archaeologist and paleoanthropologist who made several fossil finds of great importance in the understanding of human evolution. Her early finds were interpreted and publicized by her husband, the noted anthropologist Louis S.B. Leakey.

As a girl, Mary exhibited a natural talent for drawing and was interested in archaeology. After undergoing sporadic schooling, she participated in excavations of a Neolithic Period site at Hembury, Devon, England, by which time she had become skilled at making reproduction-quality

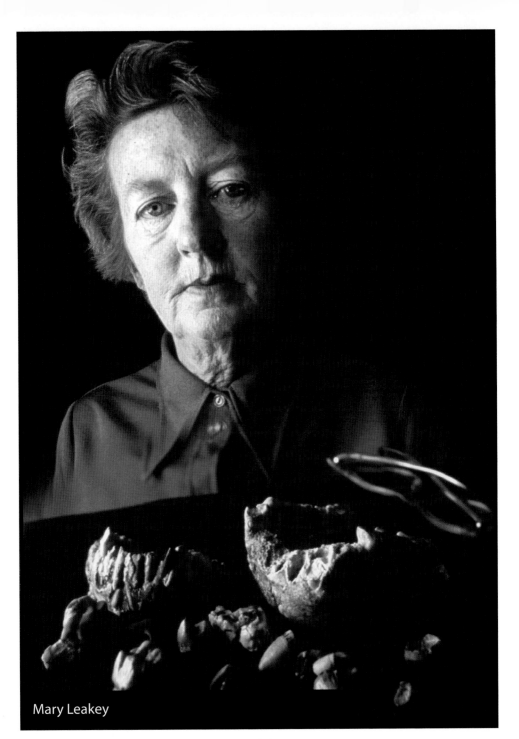
Mary Leakey

drawings of stone tools. She met Louis Leakey in 1933, and they were married in 1936. Shortly thereafter they left for an expedition to East Africa, an area that became the central location of their work.

Working alongside Louis Leakey for the next 30 years, Mary Leakey oversaw the excavation of various prehistoric sites in Kenya. Her skill at the painstaking work of excavation surpassed her husband's, whose brilliance lay in interpreting and publicizing the fossils that they uncovered. In 1948, on Rusinga Island in Lake Victoria, she discovered the skull of Proconsul africanus, an ancestor of both apes and early humans that lived about 25 million years ago. In 1959 at Olduvai Gorge, Tanzania, she discovered the skull of an early hominin (member of the human lineage) that her husband named Zinjanthropus, or "eastern man," though it is now regarded as Paranthropus, a type of australopith, or "southern ape."

After her husband's death in 1972, Leakey continued her work in Africa. In 1978 she discovered at Laetoli, a site south of Olduvai Gorge, several sets of footprints made in volcanic ash by early hominins that lived about 3.5 million years ago. The footprints indicated that their makers walked upright; this discovery pushed back the advent of human bipedalism to a date earlier than the scientific community had previously suspected. Among Mary Leakey's books were *Olduvai Gorge: My Search for Early Man* (1979) and the autobiographical *Disclosing the Past* (1984).

HENRIETTA SWAN LEAVITT

(b. 1868—d. 1921)

Henrietta Swan Leavitt was an American astronomer known for her discovery of the relationship between period and luminosity in Cepheid variables, pulsating stars that vary regularly in brightness in periods ranging from a few days to several months.

Leavitt attended Oberlin College for two years (1886–88) and then transferred to the Society for the Collegiate Instruction of Women (later Radcliffe College), from which she graduated in 1892. Following an interest aroused in her senior year, she became a volunteer assistant in the Harvard Observatory in 1895. In 1902 she received a permanent staff appointment. From the outset she was employed in the observatory's great project, begun by Edward C. Pickering, of determining the brightnesses of all measurable stars. In this work she was associated with the older Williamina Fleming and the more nearly contemporary Annie Jump Cannon.

Leavitt soon advanced from routine work to a position as head of the photographic stellar photometry department. A new phase of the work began in 1907 with Pickering's ambitious plan to ascertain photographically standardized values for stellar magnitudes. The vastly increased accuracy permitted by photographic techniques, which unlike the subjective eye were not misled by the different colors of the stars, depended upon the establishment of a basic sequence of standard magnitudes for comparison. The problem was given to Leavitt, who began with a sequence of 46 stars in the vicinity of the north celestial pole. Devising new methods of analysis, she determined their magnitudes and then those of a much larger sample in the same region, extending the scale of standard brightnesses down to the 21st magnitude. These standards were published in 1912 and 1917.

She then established secondary standard sequences of from 15 to 22 reference stars in each of 48 selected "Harvard Standard Regions" of the sky, using photographs supplied by observatories around the world. Her North Polar Sequence was adopted for the Astrographic Map of the Sky, an international project undertaken in 1913, and by the time of her death she had completely determined magnitudes for stars in 108 areas of the sky. Her system remained in general use until improved technology made possible photoelectrical measurements of far greater accuracy. One result of her work on stellar magnitudes was her discovery of 4 novas and some 2,400 variable stars, the latter figure comprising more than half of all those known even by 1930. Leavitt continued her work at the Harvard Observatory until her death.

Leavitt's outstanding achievement was her discovery in 1912 that in a certain class of variable stars, the Cepheid variables, the period of the cycle of fluctuation in brightness is highly regular and is determined by the actual luminosity of the star. The subsequent calibration of the period-luminosity curve allowed American astronomers Edwin Hubble, Harlow Shapley, and others to determine the distances of many Cepheid stars and consequently of the star clusters and galaxies in which they were observed. The most dramatic application was Hubble's use in 1924 of a Cepheid variable to determine the distance to the great nebula in Andromeda, which was the first distance measurement for a galaxy outside the Milky Way. Although it was later discovered that there are actually two different types of Cepheid variable, the same method can still be applied separately to each type.

INGE LEHMANN

(b. 1888—d. 1993)

Inge Lehmann was a Danish seismologist best known for her discovery of the inner core of Earth in 1936 by using seismic wave data. Two boundary regions, or discontinuities, are named for her: one Lehmann discontinuity occurs between Earth's inner and outer core at a depth of roughly 5,100 km (about 3,200 miles), and the other occurs at a depth of approximately 200 km (about 120 miles) beneath Earth's surface in the upper mantle.

Inge Lehmann was born to Alfred Lehmann, a psychology professor, and Ida Tørsleff. Growing up in Copenhagen, she attended a high school that treated girls and boys equally—a progressive idea at the time. In 1907 she began her study of mathematics at the University of Copenhagen, intending to obtain a candidata magisterii (cand.mag.; comparable to a master's degree). From the autumn of 1910 to December 1911, Lehmann attended Newnham College, Cambridge, but fatigue and overwork forced her return to Copenhagen.

Lehmann did not attend school between 1911 and 1918, instead serving as an actuarial assistant. She returned to the University of Copenhagen in 1918 and graduated with a cand.mag. in mathematics in 1920. She continued studying mathematics at the University of Hamburg during the fall of 1922, before taking another position as an actuarial assistant in 1923, this time working with a professor in the actuarial science department at the

University of Copenhagen. In 1925 she became an assistant to the head of the Royal Danish Geodetic Institute, and part of her work involved setting up Denmark's first seismic stations near Copenhagen, as well as in Ivigtut and Scoresbysund (now Ittoqqortoomiit), Greenland. Because of her growing interest in that topic, she again enrolled in the University of Copenhagen and studied seismology during the summer of 1927, later graduating with a magister scientiarum (master of science) in 1928. That same year Lehmann was appointed as the state geodesist and was made the head of the Seismological Department of the Royal Danish Geodetic Institute. She held the latter post until her retirement in 1953.

The bulk of Lehmann's work at the Seismological Department invlved managing the seismological stations both in Denmark and in Greenland, as well as collecting seismograph information and creating the bulletins associated with the stations. She became interested in determining the location of earthquake epicenters more accurately from the data her seismographs provided. She did so by correlating the primary seismic wave forms collected.. She was also interested in calculating the travel times of various types of seismic waves through the planet.

In 1929, while examining seismograph data collected after a large earthquake in New Zealand, Lehmann noticed that seismographs stationed in the Russian cities of Swerdlowsk (Yekaterinburg) and Irkutsk collected seismic waves with amplitudes that were higher than she had expected. She also discovered that some waves traveling away from the earthquake's focus appeared to have been "bent." It was known at the time that Earth's core deflected secondary (S) waves and some primary (P) waves—thereby creating shadow zones behind the core—as those waves traveled outward from an earthquake's focus to its antipode on the other side of the planet. In 1936, Lehmann published her findings in a paper that posited a three-shelled model of Earth's interior (which was made up of the mantle, outer core, and inner core), with seismic waves traveling through each shell at different but constant velocities. The model included Earth's core but also postulated the existence of an inner core. It was not until 1970 that advances in seismographs provided unequivocal evidence of the inner core's existence. The boundary between the inner and outer core, which occurs at a depth of roughly 5,100 km (about 3,200 miles), is known as the Lehmann discontinuity.

Lehmann is also known for researching Earth's mantle. Working with American seismologist Beno Gutenberg in 1954, she noticed the existence of a region in Earth's upper mantle in which seismic waves travel faster. That region, which spans perhaps 50 km (about 31 miles) and is also known as the Lehmann discontinuity, occurs about 200 km (120 miles) below Earth's surface.

In addition to her discoveries, Lehmann cofounded the Danish Geophysical Society (1936) and chaired the organization in 1941 and 1944. She was awarded the William Bowie Medal of the American Geophysical Union in 1971 for her contributions in the field of geophysics and received the Medal of the Seismological Society of America in 1977. The American Geophysical Union created the Inge Lehmann Medal in her honour in 1995, and, starting in 1997, it was awarded to researchers displaying "outstanding contributions to the understanding of the structure, composition, and dynamics of the Earth's mantle and core."

RITA LEVI-MONTALCINI

(b. 1909—d. 2012)

Neurologist Rita Levi-Montalcini, along with biochemist Stanley Cohen, shared the Nobel Prize for Physiology or Medicine in 1986 for her discovery of a bodily substance that stimulates and influences the growth of nerve cells. She held dual citizenship in Italy and the United States.

Levi-Montalcini was born on April 22, 1909, in Turin, Italy. She studied medicine at the University of Turin and did research there on the effects that peripheral tissues have on nerve cell growth. Forced into hiding in Florence during the German occupation of Italy (1943—45) because of her Jewish ancestry, she was not able to resume her research at Turin until after the war. In 1947 she accepted a post at Washington University, St. Louis, Missouri, with the zoologist Viktor Hamburger, who was studying the growth of nerve tissue in chick embryos.

In 1948 it was discovered in Hamburger's laboratory that a variety of mouse tumor spurred nerve growth when implanted into chick embryos.

Levi-Montalcini and Hamburger traced the effect to a substance in the tumor that they named nerve-growth factor (NGF). Levi-Montalcini further showed that the tumor caused similar cell growth in a nerve-tissue culture kept alive in the laboratory, and Stanley Cohen, who by then had joined her at Washington University, was able to isolate the NGF from the tumor. NGF was the first of many cell-growth factors to be found in the bodies of animals. It plays an important role in the growth of nerve cells and fibers in the peripheral nervous system.

Levi-Montalcini remained active in the field, working at Washington University until 1961 and afterward at the Institute of Cell Biology in Rome, Italy. In 1987 she was awarded the National Medal of Science, and an autobiographical work, *In Praise of Imperfection*, was published in 1988. In 2001 Italian prime minister Carlo Azeglio Ciampi appointed Levi-Montalcini Senator-for-Life for her outstanding contributions to science. Levi-Montalcini died on December 30, 2012, in Rome.

BARBARA JANE LISKOV

(b. 1939)

Barbara Jane Liskov is an American winner of the 2008 A.M. Turing Award, the highest honour in computer science, for her "pioneering work in the design of computer programming languages."

After she earned a bachelor's degree in mathematics in 1961 from the University of California, Berkeley, Liskov worked as a computer programmer in Massachusetts, first with the Mitre Corporation and then at Harvard University. Liskov returned to California in 1963, where she became a graduate assistant to John McCarthy and worked on his artificial intelligence projects at Stanford University. Liskov earned a master's degree (1965) and a doctorate (1968) from Stanford, becoming the first woman to be granted a doctorate in computer science in the United States.

After graduating from Stanford, Liskov returned to the Mitre Corporation (1968—72) before joining the faculty at the Massachusetts Institute of Technology (MIT), where she became the NEC Professor

Barbara Liskov at the A.M. Turing Award ceremony

of Software Science and Engineering (1986–97), the Ford Professor of Engineering (1997–), and an MIT Institute Professor (2008–).

Liskov's publications include *Abstraction and Specification in Program Development* (1986) and *Program Development in Java: Abstraction, Specification, and Object-Oriented Design* (2001), both in collaboration with John V. Guttag of MIT's computer science department.

JANE LUBCHENCO

(b. 1947)

U.S. environmental scientist and marine ecologist Jane Lubchenco became the first woman to serve as administrator of the National Ocean and Atmospheric Administration (NOAA). In 2009 she became the country's first female undersecretary for oceans and atmosphere.

Born in Denver, Colorado, on December 4, 1947, Lubchenco received a bachelor's degree in biology from Colorado College in 1969. She obtained a master's degree in zoology from the University of Washington in 1971 and a doctorate in ecology from Harvard University in 1975. Her thesis work focused on community structure in coastal rockpools. She served as an assistant professor at Harvard from 1975 to 1977. She began teaching marine biology at Oregon State University in 1977 and the following year became a research associate at the Smithsonian Institution, a position she held until 1984. Her areas of research included algal ecology, plant-herbivore and predator-prey interactions, global change community structure, and the evolutionary ecology of individuals. She continued to teach at Oregon State, receiving an endowed chair in 1995.

Lubchenco served as president of the Ecological Society of America in 1992—93. From 1998 to 2000 she was chair of the task force on the environment at the National Science Board, and from 1996 to 2000 she served as an adviser to Religion, Science, and the Environment, a cross-disciplinary partnership of scientists and religious leaders. She was president of the International Council for Science from 2002 to 2005. Lubchenco held memberships in the National Academy of Sciences (1996), the American Philosophical Society (1998), and other prestigious organizations.

Recognizing that environmental change did not come about without mass participation, Lubchenco sought ways to better inform the public of scientific issues and to bridge the gulf between researchers and the rest of the world. In a 1997 speech she proposed the idea of a social contract between scientists and society. In 1998 Lubchenco founded the Aldo Leopold Leadership Program, aimed at enhancing the ability of research scientists to communicate their findings to a general audience. In 1999 she helped to create the Communication Partnership for Science and Sea (COMPASS), an organization devoted to educating policy makers on ocean ecology. That year she also helmed the Partnership for Interdisciplinary Studies of Coastal Oceans (PISCO). In 2008—09 Lubchenco was one of the primary organizers of Climate Central, which focused on disseminating information on climate change to the public.

Jane Lubchenco

Her ability to combine passionate advocacy with pragmatism led to Lubchenco's nomination as NOAA administrator and undersecretary of commerce for oceans and atmosphere by President Barack Obama in 2008. She was confirmed in 2009 to wide approval from the scientific community.

WANGARI MAATHAI

(b. 1940—d. 2011)

K enyan politician and environmental activist Wangari Maathai was awarded the Nobel Peace Prize in 2004 for her "holistic approach to sustainable development that embraces democracy, human rights, and women's rights in particular." She became the first black African woman to achieve such an honor.

Wangari Muta Maathai was born on April 1, 1940, in Nyeri, Kenya. She attended college in the United States, receiving a bachelor's degree in biology from Mount St. Scholastica College (now Benedictine College) in 1964 and a master's degree from the University of Pittsburgh in 1966. In 1971 she completed her Ph.D. at the University of Nairobi, having the distinction of becoming the first woman in either East or Central Africa to earn a doctorate. After graduating, she began teaching in the Department of Veterinary Anatomy at the University of Nairobi, and in 1977 she became chair of the department.

Maathai was working with the National Council of Women of Kenya when she began to explore the idea that village women could improve the environment by planting trees. Her goal was twofold: to provide a fuel source for families and to slow the processes of deforestation and desertification. In 1977 she founded the Green Belt Movement to further her purpose, and by the early 21st century the organization had planted some 30 million trees. Organization members went on to start the Pan African Green Belt Network in 1986, which was dedicated to providing information about conservation and environmental improvement to world leaders. As a result of the organization's activism, similar movements were started in Tanzania, Ethiopia, Zimbabwe, and other African countries.

Wangari Maathai

Maathai's other interests included human rights, AIDS prevention, and women's issues. She often addressed these concerns at meetings of the United Nations General Assembly. In 2002 Maathai was elected to Kenya's National Assembly, and the next year she was appointed assistant minister of environment, natural resources, and wildlife. She was the author of several books, including *The Green Belt Movement: Sharing the Approach and the Experience* (1988), which detailed the history of the organization, and an autobiography, *Unbowed* (2007). In *The Challenge for Africa* (2009) she criticized Africa's ineffective leadership and prompted Africans to solve their problems without Western help. Maathai also contributed to such international periodicals as the *Los Angeles Times* and the *Guardian*. Maathai died on Sept. 25, 2011, in Nairobi, Kenya.

LYNN MARGULIS

(b. 1938—d. 2011)

Lynn Margulis was an American biologist whose serial endosymbiotic theory of eukaryotic cell development revolutionized the modern concept of how life arose on Earth.

Margulis was raised in Chicago. Intellectually precocious, she graduated with a bachelor's degree from the University of Chicago in 1957. Soon after, she married American astronomer Carl Sagan, with whom she had two children; one, Dorion, would become her frequent collaborator. The couple divorced in 1964. Margulis earned a master's degree in zoology and genetics from the University of Wisconsin at Madison in 1960 and a Ph.D. in genetics from the University of California, Berkeley, in 1965. She joined the biology department of Boston University in 1966 and taught there until 1988, when she was named distinguished university professor in the department of botany at the University of Massachusetts at Amherst. She retained that title when her affiliation at the university changed to the department of biology in 1993 and then to the department of geosciences in 1997.

Throughout most of her career, Margulis was considered a radical by peers who pursued traditional Darwinian "survival of the fittest" approaches to biology. Her ideas, which focused on symbiosis—a living arrangement of two different organisms in an association that can be either beneficial or unfavourable—were frequently greeted with skepticism and even hostility. Among her most important work was the development of the serial endosymbiotic theory (SET) of the origin of cells, which posits that eukaryotic cells (cells with nuclei) evolved from the symbiotic merger of nonnucleated bacteria that had previously existed independently. In this theory, mitochondria and chloroplasts, two major organelles of eukaryotic cells, are descendants of once free-living bacterial species. She explained the concept in her first book, *Origin of Eukaryotic Cells* (1970). At the time, her theory was regarded as far-fetched, but it has since been widely accepted. She elaborated in her 1981 classic, *Symbiosis in Cell Evolution*, proposing that another symbiotic merger of cells with bacteria—this time spirochetes, a type of bacterium that undulates rapidly—developed into the internal transportation system of the nucleated cell. Margulis further postulated that eukaryotic cilia were also originally spirochetes and that cytoplasm evolved from a symbiotic relationship between eubacteria and archaebacteria.

Her 1982 book *Five Kingdoms*, written with American biologist Karlene V. Schwartz, articulates a five-kingdom system of classifying life on Earth—animals, plants, bacteria (prokaryotes), fungi, and protoctists. The protist kingdom, which comprises most unicellular organisms (and multicellular algae) in other systems, is rejected as too general. Many of the organisms usually categorized as protists are placed in one of the other four kingdoms; protoctists make up the remaining organisms, which are all aquatic, and include algae and slime molds. Margulis edited portions of the compendium *Handbook of Protoctista* (1990).

Another area of interest for Margulis was her long collaboration with British scientist James Lovelock on the controversial Gaia hypothesis. This proposes that the Earth can be viewed as a single self-regulating organism—that is, a complex entity whose living and inorganic elements are interdependent and whose life-forms actively modify the environment to maintain hospitable conditions.

In addition to Margulis's scholarly publications, she wrote numerous books interpreting scientific concepts and quandaries for a popular audience. Among them were *Mystery Dance: On the Evolution of Human Sexuality* (1991), *What Is Life?* (1995), *What Is Sex?* (1997), and *Dazzle Gradually: Reflections on Nature in Nature* (2007), all cowritten with her son. She also wrote a book of stories, *Luminous Fish* (2007). Her later efforts were published under the Sciencewriters Books imprint of Chelsea Green Publishing, which she cofounded with Dorion in 2006.

Margulis was elected to the National Academy of Sciences in 1983 and was one of three American members of the Russian Academy of Natural Sciences. She was awarded the William Procter Prize of Sigma Xi, an international research society, and the U.S. National Medal of Science in 1999. In 2008 she received the Darwin-Wallace Medal of the Linnean Society of London. She was a coauthor, with Dorion, of Encyclopædia Britannica's article on life.

MARIA GOEPPERT MAYER

(b. 1906—d. 1972)

The German-American physicist Maria Goeppert Mayer won the 1963 Nobel Prize for Physics with J. Hans Daniel Jensen and Eugene P. Wigner. They were awarded the prize for their explanation of the structure and properties of atomic nuclei.

Maria Goeppert was born in Kattowitz, Germany, on June 28, 1906. Her father was professor of pediatrics at Göttingen University. She studied theoretical physics at the university under Max Born and earned her doctorate in 1930. In the same year, she married Joseph E. Mayer, an American chemical physicist, and they moved to the United States to teach at Johns Hopkins University.

In 1939 she began teaching at Sarah Lawrence College and at Columbia University, where she worked on the separation of uranium isotopes for the atomic bomb in the Manhattan Project. In 1945 she continued her research at the University of Chicago's Institute for Nuclear Studies and at the nearby Argonne National Laboratory. Mayer explained the great abundance and stability of nuclei that have a particular number of protons and neutrons in terms of the so-called nuclear shell theory. Her findings were published in "Elementary Theory of Nuclear Shell Structure" (1955), coauthored by Jensen. In 1960 Mayer and her husband moved to the University of California at San Diego. She died there on Feb. 20, 1972.

BARBARA McCLINTOCK
(b. 1902—d. 1992)

In the 1940s and 1950s American geneticist Barbara McClintock discovered that chromosomes can break off from neighboring chromosomes and recombine to create unique genetic combinations in a process known as crossing over, a radical break from accepted genetic doctrine of the time. The importance of her research, performed on corn (maize), was not recognized for many years. Only after geneticists found other movable genetic elements, such as transposons, in both plants and animals was McClintock acknowledged for her role in explaining complicated patterns of inheritance. She was awarded the 1983 Nobel Prize for Physiology or Medicine, the first woman ever to win an unshared prize in that category.

Barbara McClintock was born on June 16, 1902, in Hartford, Conn., and was reared in New York City. She earned her doctorate in botany at Cornell University in 1927, and remained there until 1941 to do research work with the "Cornell corn group" of R.A. Emerson, George Beadle, Marcus Rhoades, and Charles Burnham. At the end of 1941 she began her long association with the Cold Spring Harbor Laboratory in Long Island, N.Y., where she worked in almost total isolation for 50 years.

Despite her maverick reputation she garnered many honors, including the National Medal of Science in 1970, and she became president of the Genetics Society in 1945. At the time of her death on Sept. 2, 1992, in Huntington, N.Y., many of her colleagues agreed that she was "one of the three Ms": Gregor Mendel, Thomas Hunt Morgan, and Barbara McClintock—the most important figures in the history of genetics.

MARGARET MEAD

(b. 1901—d. 1978)

With the publication in 1928 of her first book, *Coming of Age in Samoa*, Margaret Mead began to establish her reputation as one of the foremost anthropologists of the 20th century. She was also a popular and controversial speaker on such contemporary social issues as women's rights, child rearing, drug abuse, population control, and world hunger. As an anthropologist, Mead published extensively on peoples of the South Pacific.

Mead was born on December 16, 1901, in Philadelphia, Pennsylvania. She received her master's degree in psychology from Barnard College in 1924 and earned her doctorate at Columbia University under anthropologist Franz Boas. While at Columbia she made the first of several trips to the South Pacific in 1925—26. She became assistant curator of ethnology at the American Museum of Natural History in New York in 1926 and remained with the museum until 1969, the last five years as curator. From 1954 until retirement she taught anthropology at Columbia and chaired the social sciences division of Fordham University (1968—71). She died in New York City on November 15, 1978. The following year she was posthumously awarded the Presidential Medal of Freedom.

Coming of Age has remained in print since its first publication. Among Mead's other books are *Growing Up in New Guinea* (1930) and *Sex and Temperament in Three Primitive Societies* (1935). She analyzed American cultural standards in *And Keep Your Powder Dry* in 1942.

One of her most significant later publications was *Male and Female* (1949). Her autobiography, *Blackberry Winter*, was published in 1972.

LISE MEITNER

(b. 1878—d. 1968)

The Austrian physicist Lise Meitner shared the Enrico Fermi Award in 1966 with Otto Hahn and Fritz Strassmann for research leading to the discovery of nuclear fission. Her own primary work in physics dealt with the relation between beta and gamma rays.

Meitner was born in Vienna on Nov. 7, 1878. She studied at the University of Vienna, where she received her doctorate in physics in 1907. She then went to Berlin to join chemist Otto Hahn in research on radioactivity. She studied with Max Planck and worked as his assistant.

In 1913 Meitner became a member of the Kaiser Wilhelm Institute in Berlin (now the Max Planck Institute). In 1917 she became head of its physics section and codirector with Otto Hahn. They worked together for about 30 years and discovered and named protactinium. They also investigated the products of neutron bombardment of uranium.

Because she was Jewish, Meitner fled Germany in 1938 to escape Nazi persecution. She went to Sweden, which remained neutral during World War II. Here, with her nephew Otto Frisch, she studied the physical characteristics of neutron-bombarded uranium and proposed the name fission for the process. Hahn and Strassmann, following the same line of research, noted that the bombardment produced much lighter elements. Later advances in the study of nuclear fission led to nuclear weapons and nuclear power. In 1960 Meitner retired to live in England. She died in Cambridge on Oct. 27, 1968.

MARIA SIBYLLA MERIAN

(b. 1647—d. 1717)

Maria Sibylla Merian was a German-born naturalist and nature artist known for her illustrations of insects and plants. Her works on insect development and the transformation of insects through the process of metamorphosis contributed to the advance of entomology in the late 17th and early 18th centuries.

When Merian was three, her father, renowned illustrator Matthäus Merian, died, and she subsequently was raised by her mother and stepfather, still-life painter Jacob Marrel. Merian studied painting under the tutelage of Marrel at the family's Frankfurt home. She collected insects and other specimens for Marrel's compositions, and in these formative years, nature—plants and caterpillars in particular—became Merian's primary subjects of artistic interest. She eventually started her own caterpillar collection in order to study the insects' maturation into butterflies. Even in these early years of her career, Merian's observations and illustrations of insects and plants in various life stages were remarkable for their scientific quality.

In 1665 Merian married Johann Andreas Graff, an apprentice of Marrel's. Three years later, the couple's first daughter, Johanna Helena, was born, and soon after the family moved to Nürnberg, Graff's hometown. They remained there for the next 14 years, during which time Merian created a series of watercolor engravings of popular flowers. These illustrations were published between 1675 and 1680 in the three-volume *Blumenbuch* ("Book of Flowers"), which was later reprinted, with 36 plates and a preface, as *Neues Blumenbuch* ("New Book of Flowers"). In 1678 the couple's second daughter, Dorothea Maria, was born. The following year, Merian published the first volume of *Der Raupen wunderbare Verwandelung, und sonderbare Blumen-nahrung* ("Caterpillars, Their Wondrous Transformation and Peculiar Nourishment from Flowers"; the second volume appeared in 1683), in which she depicted in detail the metamorphosis of moths and butterflies. Each insect was shown on or beside its plant food source and was accompanied by text describing the stage of metamorphosis illustrated. The work was celebrated for its scientific accuracy and for bringing a new standard of precision to scientific illustration.

Merian, Graff, and their children eventually returned to Frankfurt, apparently to care for Merian's mother following her stepfather's death in 1681. In 1685, however, Graff returned, alone, to Nürnberg, and the next year Merian, her mother, and her daughters set out for the village of

Wiewert (Wieuwerd) in West Friesland (now in the Netherlands), where her half-brother Caspar had joined a Labadist colony (Labadists were a separatist group of Pietists founded by theologian Jean de Labadie). During her time with the colony, Merian appears to have produced few paintings. In 1691, a year after her mother's death, Merian and her daughters went to Amsterdam. She soon after was legally divorced from Graff.

In 1699 Merian and Dorothea Maria set sail for a projected five-year-long expedition to Suriname, located on the northern coast of South America. The voyage afforded Merian a unique opportunity to explore new species of insects and plants. The two women settled in at Paramaribo and together collected, studied, and composed illustrations of the jungle's plants, insects, and other animals. After less than two years, however, illness forced Merian to return to Amsterdam. In 1705 she published *Metamorphosis insectorum Surinamensium* ("The Metamorphosis of the Insects of Suriname"). Arguably the most important work of her career, it included some 60 engravings illustrating the different stages of development that she had observed in Suriname's insects. Similar to her caterpillar book, *Metamorphosis* depicted the insects on and around their host plants and included text describing each stage of development. The book was one of the first illustrated accounts of the natural history of Suriname.

The year of Merian's death, her paintings were purchased for Peter I, tsar of Russia. Dorothea Maria subsequently was summoned to St. Petersburg, where she worked as a scientific illustrator for the tsar and became the first woman to be employed by the Russian Academy of Sciences. Johanna Helena, who moved with her husband to Suriname in 1711, likewise became a noted artist in her own right.

MARYAM MIRZAKHANI

(b. 1977)

Maryam Mirzakhani is an Iranian mathematician who became, in 2014, the first woman and the first Iranian to be awarded a Fields Medal. The citation for her award recognized "her outstanding contributions to the dynamics and geometry of Riemann surfaces and their moduli spaces."

While a teenager, Mirzakhani won gold medals in the 1994 and 1995 International Mathematical Olympiads for high-school students, attaining a perfect score in 1995. In 1999 she received a B.Sc. degree in mathematics from the Sharif University of Technology in Tehran. Five years later she earned a Ph.D. from Harvard University for her dissertation "Simple Geodesics on Hyperbolic Surfaces and Volume of the Moduli Space of Curves." Mirzakhani served (2004–08) as a Clay Mathematics Institute research fellow and an assistant professor of mathematics at Princeton University. In 2008 she became a professor at Stanford University.

Mirzakhani's work focused on the study of hyperbolic surfaces by means of their moduli spaces. In hyperbolic space, in contrast with normal Euclidean space, Euclid's fifth postulate (that one and only one line parallel to a given line can pass through a fixed point) does not hold. In non-Euclidean hyperbolic space, an infinite number of parallel lines can pass through such a fixed point. The sum of the angles of a triangle in hyperbolic space is less than 180°. In such a curved space, the shortest path between two points is known as a geodesic. For example, on a sphere the geodesic is a great circle. Mirzakhani's research involved calculating the number of a certain type of geodesic, called simple closed geodesics, on hyperbolic surfaces.

Her technique involved considering the moduli spaces of the surfaces. In this case the modulus space is a collection of all Riemann spaces that have a certain characteristic. Mirzakhani found that a property of the modulus space corresponds to the number of simple closed geodesics of the hyperbolic surface.

MARIA MITCHELL

(b. 1818—d. 1889)

The first professional woman astronomer in the United States was Maria Mitchell. Her interest in science and mathematics, encouraged by her father, led her to become a self-taught astronomer.

Mitchell was born on the Massachusetts island of Nantucket on Aug. 1, 1818. Beginning as a teenager, she worked during the day as a librarian at Nantucket's Atheneum and taught herself astronomy by reading books on mathematics and science. At night she regularly studied the sky through her father's telescope. In October 1847 her discovery of a comet brought her worldwide attention, and a year later she became the first woman to be elected to the American Academy of Arts and Sciences.

In 1865 Mitchell was appointed professor of astronomy at Vassar College in Poughkeepsie, N.Y., and director of the observatory there. In 1873 she helped found the Association for the Advancement of Women. She was a pioneer in the daily photography of sunspots and was the first to discover that they were not clouds but whirling vortices of gas on the sun's surface. She also studied solar eclipses, double stars, nebulas, and the satellites of Saturn and Jupiter.

Mitchell died in Lynn, Mass., on June 28, 1889. In 1905 she was one of the first women elected to the Hall of Fame. An observatory was erected in her honor on Nantucket Island.

CLELIA DUEL MOSHER

(b. 1863—d. 1940)

Clelia Duel Mosher was a U.S. doctor and researcher. Although a wealth of public information about women's bodies and sexuality was available by the late 20th century, such topics were rarely written about or discussed when Clelia D. Mosher began practicing medicine in the early 1900s. Mosher's studies dared to demystify female physiology, and her writings were among the first to cover topics such as menstruation and menopause.

Mosher was born on Dec. 16, 1863, in Albany, N.Y. Her father and several uncles were physicians, and pioneer woman physician Eliza Mosher was a distant cousin. Her plans to attend college after finishing preparatory school were discouraged by her father, who was grieving the death of his other daughter and felt Mosher herself was still too weak from a bout of tuberculosis. Mosher instead trained as a florist, and by age 25, she saved enough money from working to pay for schooling at Wellesley College in Massachusetts. Illness forced her to interrupt her education, but she resumed it at the University of Wisconsin. She transferred to Stanford University in California for her senior year and earned a bachelor's degree in 1893. She became an assistant in the girls' gymnasium at Stanford and was granted a master's degree in 1894 for her research on the breathing habits of women. Her findings disputed the commonly held notion that women naturally breathe from the upper part of their chests.

Mosher graduated from Johns Hopkins Medical School in 1900. She returned to Palo Alto, Calif., and built up a practice treating women and children. After ten years, she longed to return to academia and became a professor of personal hygiene and the medical adviser for women at Stanford. She retired in 1929.

Mosher authored the books *Health and the Woman Movement* (1916), *Woman's Physical Freedom* (1923), and *Personal Hygiene for Women* (1927). She blamed constrictive corsets for many menstrual problems and was one of the first people to suggest menopause may be less psychologically trying on women who have interests outside of homemaking. Her writings also touted such things as good nutrition, regular exercise, and wearing clothing that would not interfere with normal breathing.

FLORENCE NIGHTINGALE

(b. 1820—d. 1910)

In 1854 the English nurse Florence Nightingale took a small band of volunteers to Turkey to care for soldiers wounded in the Crimean War. There she coped with conditions of crowding, poor sanitation, and shortage of basic supplies. After the war she established nursing as a profession and devoted the rest of her life to improving hospital care.

Florence Nightingale was born on May 12, 1820, to well-to-do parents at their temporary residence in Florence, Italy. Named for her birthplace, she grew up in Derbyshire, Hampshire, and London, where her family maintained temporary homes. Nightingale was educated largely by her father. After her parents refused her request to study nursing at a hospital, Nightingale was persuaded to study parliamentary reports. In three years she was an expert on public health and hospitals.

Over her parents' objections she visited hospitals in England and continental Europe. In 1846 a friend sent her the Year Book of the Institution of Protestant Deaconesses at Kaiserswerth, Germany. Four years later Nightingale entered that same institution and was trained as a nurse. In 1853 she was appointed superintendent of the Institution for the Care of Sick Gentlewomen, in London.

When war with Russia broke out, Nightingale volunteered her services. She was appointed head of the nurses in the military hospitals in Scutari, Turkey. When she arrived more men were dying from fever and infection than from battle wounds. One of Nightingale's first requests was for scrubbing brushes. She enforced sanitary regulations, introduced special diets, and reduced the death rate from 45 to 2 percent. With her own money she bought linen, shirts, food, and even beds for the hospitals. Her health broke. She contracted Crimean fever and nearly died. But she refused to return to England.

By 1856 Florence Nightingale was world famous. She returned to England and met with Queen Victoria and other dignitaries to persuade them to improve conditions for the British soldier. From 1857 she lived as an invalid.

England gave her 50,000 pounds in 1860, which she used to establish the Nightingale School for Nurses. She campaigned by letter for hospital reforms, enforced high professional standards in caring for the sick, and established nursing as a respectable career for women. Nightingale died on August 13, 1910, in London.

EMMY NOETHER

(b. 1882—d. 1935)

Recognized as one of the most creative abstract algebraists of modern times, Emmy Noether developed an abstract theory that drew together many mathematical developments. She brought startling innovations to higher algebra. The German mathematician's areas of research include the general theory of ideals and the application of non-commutative algebras to commutative number fields.

Amalie Emmy Noether was born in Erlangen, Germany, on March 23, 1882. Her father, Max Noether, was a professor of mathematics. She received a Ph.D. from the University of Erlangen in 1907, with a dissertation on algebraic invariants. She lectured at the university beginning in 1913, occasionally substituting for her father. In 1915 she went to the University of Göttingen. Despite the objections of some faculty members, Noether was formally admitted as an academic lecturer in 1919.

Noether first gained recognition when her work was published in Mathematische Zeitschrift in 1920. For the next six years she focused on the general theory of ideals (special subsets of rings), for which her residual theorem is an important part. Beginning in 1927 she concentrated on noncommutative algebras, or the algebras in which the order in which the numbers are multiplied affects the answer. She built up the theory of noncommutative algebras in a newly unified and purely conceptual way. In collaboration with Helmut Hasse and Richard Brauer, she investigated the structure of noncommutative algebras and their application to commutative fields by means of cross product (a form of multiplication used between two vectors).

From 1930 to 1933 she was the center of the strongest mathematical activity at Göttingen. The extent and significance of her work cannot be accurately judged from her papers. Much of her work appeared in the publications of students and colleagues, and many times a suggestion or even a casual remark revealed her great insight and stimulated another to complete and perfect some idea. Noether helped edit the *Mathematische Annalen*, but she was dismissed along with other Jewish professors when the Nazis came to power in 1933. She and her Jewish colleagues were also dismissed from their posts at the university.

That year she left for the United States to become a visiting professor of mathematics at Bryn Mawr College in Pennsylvania. While she taught at Bryn Mawr, she also lectured and conducted research at the Institute for Advanced Study in Princeton, New Jersey. Noether died on April 14, 1935, in Bryn Mawr, Pennsylvania.

ANTONIA NOVELLO

(b. 1944)

U.S. physician and public official Antonia Novello was both the first Hispanic and the first woman to become surgeon general of the United States. Her major initiatives included programs to increase AIDS awareness, to stop minors from smoking, and to provide better health care for children, women, and minorities.

She was born Antonia Coello on Aug. 23, 1944, in Fajardo, Puerto Rico. After undergoing surgery at age 18 to correct a serious colon condition that she had had since birth, Novello was inspired to become a physician so that she could help ease the suffering of other young people. She studied medicine at the University of Puerto Rico, where she earned her B.S. degree in 1965 and her M.D. degree in 1970. After medical school she married a Navy flight surgeon named Joseph R. Novello, and the couple soon moved to Ann Arbor, Mich., where she began her medical career. Novello completed a pediatric internship and residency and a fellowship in pediatric nephrology at the University of Michigan Medical Center. She went on to complete another pediatric fellowship in 1974—75 at Georgetown University Hospital. Novello broadened her education in 1982 when she earned a master's degree in public health from Johns Hopkins University.

After venturing into private practice as a pediatrician in Springfield, Va., Novello joined the staff of the National Institutes of Health (NIH) in 1978. She played a critical role in the development of the Organ Transplantation Procurement Act of 1984 and also served as a fellow on the staff of the Senate's Labor and Human Resources Committee. In that position Novello consulted with legislators on bills concerning various health issues, including organ transplants and the warnings on cigarette packages. In 1986 she became the deputy director of the National Institute of Child Health and Human Development and the following year became its coordinator for AIDS research.

In 1990 Novello was appointed surgeon general of the United States by President George Bush. During her three years in that post, Novello was a strong advocate for children's health issues. She worked with several organizations to promote the immunization of children and the prevention of childhood injuries and was involved with the Healthy Children Ready to Learn Initiative. She was especially active in the fight against illegal alcohol and tobacco use among minors—denouncing, for example, the tobacco industry's use of cartoon characters such as "Joe Camel" to try to make smoking more appealing to young people.

In 1993 Novello stepped down from the post of surgeon general, but she continued to advocate for children's health issues by becoming the Special Representative for Health and Nutrition for the United Nations Children's Fund (UNICEF). She returned to Johns Hopkins University in 1996 as a visiting professor. In 1999 Novello became commissioner of the New York State Department of Health, addressing such local issues as protecting residents against the West Nile virus, providing better care for nursing home residents, and providing health care coverage for uninsured residents with low incomes.

CHRISTIANE NÜSSLEIN-VOLHARD

(b. 1942)

German developmental geneticist Christiane Nüsslein-Volhard won the Nobel Prize for Physiology or Medicine in 1995 for making significant contributions to the study of how living things develop from embryos into adults. She shared the prize with geneticists Eric F. Wieschaus and Edward B. Lewis. Nüsslein-Volhard, working with Wieschaus, expanded upon the pioneering work of Lewis, who used the fruit fly (Drosophila melanogaster) as an experimental subject.

Nüsslein-Volhard was born on October 20, 1942, in Magdeburg, Germany. She attended the Goethe University Frankfurt am Main before transferring to the Eberhard-Karl University of Tübingen to take part in a new curriculum in biochemistry, the first of its kind in Germany. She earned a diploma in biochemistry in 1968 and a doctorate in genetics in 1973. Searching for a postdoctoral project, she came upon the fruit fly, which had been used by other scientists to study genetic mutations.

Christiane Nüsslein-Volhard

Because the fruit fly developed from fertilized egg to embryo in nine days and its genetic structure was similar to that of humans, it was an ideal research subject.

After holding fellowships in Basel, Switzerland, and Freiburg, East Germany (now Germany), Nüsslein-Volhard joined Wieschaus as a group leader at the European Molecular Biology Laboratory in Heidelberg, West Germany (now Germany). There the two scientists spent more than a year crossbreeding 40,000 fruit fly families and systematically examining their genetic makeup. Their trial-and-error methods resulted in the discovery that of the fly's 20,000 genes, about 5,000 are deemed important to early development and about 140 are essential. Nüsslein-Volhard and Wieschaus published their findings in the English scientific journal *Nature* in 1980.

Nüsslein-Volhard and Wieschaus's discovery had an immediate and dramatic effect on developmental biology. The two had established for the first time that genes controlling development could be individually identified, which encouraged scientists to search for developmental genes in other species, including humans. Using the fruit fly experiments as a blueprint, scientists were able to identify the genes in humans responsible for causing various birth defects.

In 1981 Nüsslein-Volhard returned to Tübingen, where, in 1985, she became director of the Max Planck Institute for Developmental Biology. She continued to experiment in developmental genetics and published papers on the subject throughout the early 21st century. In addition to her Drosophila experiments, Nüsslein-Volhard investigated the genetic development of the zebra fish (Danio rerio) and sought to use it as a model for vertebrate development.

In addition to the Nobel Prize, Nüsslein-Volhard received the Leibniz Prize in 1986 and the Albert Lasker Basic Medical Research Award in 1991. She also published several books, including *Zebrafish: A Practical Approach* (2002; written with Ralf Dahm) and *Coming to Life: How Genes Drive Development* (2006).

ELLEN OCHOA

(b. 1958)

American engineer Ellen Ochoa was the first Hispanic female astronaut, serving on four space shuttle flights. She also helped develop several systems that use lasers to gather and process information from images.

Ochoa was born on May 10, 1958, in Los Angeles, California. She studied electrical engineering at Stanford University, earning a master's degree in 1981 and a doctorate in 1985. She also played the flute with the Stanford Symphony Orchestra. A specialist in the development of optical systems, Ochoa worked as a research engineer at Sandia National Laboratories. She later designed computer systems at the Ames Research Center of the National Aeronautics and Space Administration (NASA).

Ellen Ochoa

In 1990 Ochoa was selected by NASA to participate in its astronaut program, and she completed her training the following year. In 1993 she served as mission specialist aboard the space shuttle *Discovery*, becoming the first Hispanic woman to travel into space. She took part in an *Atlantis* mission in 1994, and in 1999 she was a member of the *Discovery* crew that executed the first docking to the International Space Station (ISS). Ochoa returned to the ISS aboard the *Atlantis* in 2002. She later served as the deputy director of the Johnson Space Center in Houston, Texas.

CECILIA PAYNE-GAPOSCHKIN
(b. 1900—d. 1979)

British-born American astronomer Cecilia Payne-Gaposchkin discovered that stars are made mainly of hydrogen and helium and established that stars could be classified according to their temperatures.

Payne entered the University of Cambridge in 1919. A lecture by astronomer Sir Arthur Eddington on his expedition to the island of Principe that confirmed Einstein's theory of general relativity inspired her to become an astronomer. Eddington encouraged her ambition, but she felt there were more opportunities for a woman to work in astronomy in the United States than in Britain. In 1923 she received a fellowship to study at the Harvard College Observatory in Cambridge, Mass., after a correspondence with its director, Harlow Shapley.

Beginning in the 1880s, astronomers at Harvard College such as Edward Pickering, Annie Jump Cannon, Williamina Fleming, and Antonia Maury had succeeded in classifying stars according to their spectra into seven types: O, B, A, F, G, K, and M. It was believed that this sequence corresponded to the surface temperature of the stars, with O being the hottest and M the coolest. In her Ph.D. thesis (published as *Stellar Atmospheres* [1925]), Payne used the spectral lines of many different elements and the work of Indian astrophysicist Meghnad Saha, who had discovered an equation relating the ionization states of an element in a star to the temperature to definitively establish that the spectral sequence did correspond to quantifiable stellar temperatures. Payne also determined that stars are composed mostly of hydrogen and helium. However, she was dissuaded from this conclusion by astronomer Henry Norris Russell, who thought that stars would have the same composition as Earth. (Russell conceded in 1929 that Payne was correct.) Payne received the first Ph.D. in astronomy from Radcliffe College for her thesis, since Harvard did not grant doctoral degrees to women. Astronomers Otto Struve and Velta Zebergs later called her thesis "undoubtedly the most brilliant Ph.D. thesis ever written in astronomy."

Payne remained at Harvard as a technical assistant to Shapley after completing her doctorate. Shapley had her discontinue her work with stellar spectra and encouraged her instead to work on photometry of stars by using photographic plates, even though more accurate brightness measurements could be made by using recently introduced photoelectric instruments. Payne later wrote, "I wasted much time on this account.... My change in field made the end of the decade a sad one." During this period, however, Payne was able to continue her stellar spectral work with a second book, *Stars of High Luminosity* (1930), which paid particular attention to Cepheid variables and marked the beginning of her interest in variable stars and novae.

In 1933 Payne traveled to Europe to meet Russian astronomer Boris Gerasimovich, who had previously worked at the Harvard College Observatory and with whom she planned to write a book about variable stars. In Göttingen, Ger., she met Sergey Gaposchkin, a Russian astronomer who could not return to the Soviet Union because of his politics. Payne was able to find a position at Harvard for him. They married in 1934 and often collaborated on studies of variable stars. She was named a lecturer in astronomy in 1938, but even though she taught courses, they were not listed in the Harvard catalog until after World War II.

In 1956 Payne was appointed a full professor at Harvard and became chairman of the astronomy department. She retired in 1966. She wrote an autobiography, *The Dyer's Hand*, that was posthumously collected in *Cecilia Payne-Gaposchkin: An Autobiography and Other Recollections* (1984).

DIXY LEE RAY

(b. 1914—d. 1994)

A merican zoologist and government official Dixy Lee Ray was a colorful and outspoken supporter of the nuclear industry, critic of the environmental movement, and proponent of making science more accessible to the public.

A childhood fascination with the sea led to bachelor's (1937) and master's (1938) degrees in zoology from Mills College, Oakland, California. After teaching biology in Oakland for several years, Ray enrolled at Stanford University, where she earned a doctorate in zoology (1945). A specialist in marine crustacea, Ray then joined the faculty of the University of Washington, where she taught for 27 years. In 1963 Ray accepted the directorship of the Pacific Science Center in Seattle, having previously consulted for the National Science Foundation (1960 – 62). She developed the center into a major facility for publicizing and popularizing science.

Although she had served on numerous federal advisory groups, Ray first moved to Washington, D.C., in August 1972 after she was selected by Pres. Richard Nixon to be a member of the Atomic Energy Commission (AEC). The first woman to be appointed to a full five-year term, she succeeded James Schlesinger as chairman of that body the following year. Ray's unconventional lifestyle (she lived in a house trailer with her two dogs, which occasionally accompanied her to the office) provided piquant contrast to the stereotypical Washington bureaucracy. Following the fracture of the AEC into two agencies in 1974, Ray moved to the Department of State and served as assistant secretary in charge of the Bureau of Oceans, International Environmental and Scientific Affairs. She resigned in 1975, protesting a lack of support from Secretary of State Henry A. Kissinger, and returned to Washington state.

Ray was elected governor of Washington in 1977 and served one four-year term. Her increasingly conservative policies, in tandem with a combative relationship with the press, led to her defeat in the 1980 Democratic primary.

In addition to writing many scientific papers, Ray was coauthor of two books on what she considered to be the excesses of the environmental movement—*Trashing the Planet* (1990) and *Environmental Overkill* (1993). While conservative commentators took the message of those volumes as a rallying cry against what they perceived as alarmist attitudes toward environmental problems such as global warming, critics in the scientific community excoriated Ray for misrepresenting scientific studies to suit her arguments.

ELLEN SWALLOW RICHARDS

(b. 1842—d. 1911)

Ellen Swallow Richards was an American chemist and founder of the home economics movement in the United States.

Ellen Swallow was educated mainly at home. She briefly attended Westford Academy and also taught school for a time. Swallow was trained as a chemist, earning an A.B. from Vassar College in 1870 and, as the first woman admitted to the Massachusetts Institute of Technology (MIT), a B.S. in 1873. Vassar accepted her master's thesis the same year. She remained at MIT for two more years of graduate studies, but she was not awarded a Ph.D. In 1875 she married Robert Hallowell Richards, an expert in mining and metallurgy at MIT.

In November 1876, at her urging, the Woman's Education Association of Boston contributed funds for the opening of a Woman's Laboratory at MIT. There, as assistant director under Professor John M. Ordway, she began her work of encouraging women to enter the sciences and of providing opportunities for scientific training to capable and interested women. Courses in basic and industrial chemistry, biology, and mineralogy were taught, and through Ordway a certain amount of industrial and government consulting work was obtained. Richards published several books and pamphlets as a result of her work with the Woman's Laboratory, including *The Chemistry of Cooking and Cleaning* (1882; with Marion Talbot) and *Food Materials and Their Adulterations* (1885).

From 1876 Richards was also head of the science section of the Society to Encourage Studies at Home. In 1881, with Alice Freeman Palmer and others, she was a founder of the Association of Collegiate Alumnae (later the American Association of University Women). The Woman's Laboratory closed in 1883, by which time its students had been regularly admitted to MIT. In 1884 Richards became assistant to Professor William R. Nichols in the institute's new laboratory of sanitation chemistry, and she held the post of instructor on the MIT faculty for the rest of her life. During 1887—89 she had charge of laboratory work for the Massachusetts State Board of Health's survey of inland waters.

In 1890, under Richards's guidance, the New England Kitchen was opened in Boston to offer to working-class families nutritious food, scientifically prepared at low cost, and at the same time to demonstrate the methods employed. From 1894 the Boston School Committee obtained school lunches from the New England Kitchen. Richards lobbied for the introduction of courses in domestic science into the public schools of Boston, and in 1897 she helped Mary M.K. Kehew organize a school of housekeeping in the Woman's Educational and Industrial Union that was later taken over by Simmons College. In 1899 Richards called a summer conference of workers in the fledgling field of domestic science at Lake Placid, New York. Under her chairmanship the series of such conferences held over the next several years established standards, course outlines, bibliographies, and women's club study guides for the field, for which the name "home economics" was adopted. In December 1908 the Lake Placid conferees formed the American Home Economics Association, of which Richards was elected first president. She held the post until her retirement in 1910, and in that time she established the association's *Journal of Home Economics.* In 1910 she was named to the council of the National Education Association with primary responsibility for overseeing the teaching of home economics in public schools. Among her other published works were *Home Sanitation: A Manual for Housekeepers* (1887), *Domestic Economy as a Factor in Public Education* (1889), *The Cost of Living* (1899), *Sanitation in Daily Life* (1907), and *Euthenics: The Science of Controllable Environment* (1912).

SALLY RIDE

(b. 1951—d. 2012)

In 1983 the astronaut Sally Ride became the first American woman to travel into space. Only two other women preceded her into space: Valentina Tereshkova (in 1963) and Svetlana Savitskaya (in 1982), both from the former Soviet Union.

Sally Kristen Ride was born on May 26, 1951, in Encino, California. She showed great early promise as a tennis player, but

Sally Ride on the space shuttle orbiter *Challenger*

she eventually gave up her plans to play professionally and attended Stanford University. She graduated in 1973 with bachelor's degrees in English and physics. In 1978, as a doctoral candidate and teaching assistant in laser physics at Stanford, she was selected by the National Aeronautics and Space Administration (NASA) as one of six women astronaut candidates. Ride received a Ph.D. in astrophysics and began her training and evaluation courses that same year. In August 1979 she completed her NASA training, obtained a pilot's license, and became eligible for assignment as a U.S. space shuttle mission specialist.

On June 18, 1983, Ride became the first American woman in space while rocketing into orbit aboard the space shuttle *Challenger*. The shuttle mission lasted six days, during which time she helped deploy two communications satellites and carry out a variety of experiments. She served on a second space mission aboard *Challenger* in October 1984. The crew included another woman, Ride's childhood friend Kathryn Sullivan, who became the first American woman to walk in space.

Ride was training for a third shuttle mission when the *Challenger* exploded after launch in January 1986, a catastrophe that caused NASA to suspend shuttle flights for more than two years. Ride served on the presidential commission appointed to investigate the accident. She repeated that role as a member of the commission that investigated the in-flight breakup of the shuttle *Columbia* in February 2003.

Ride resigned from NASA in 1987, and in 1989 she became a professor of physics at the University of California, San Diego, and director of its California Space Institute (until 1996). In 1999–2000 she held executive positions with Space.com, a Web site presenting space, astronomy, and technology content. From the 1990s Ride initiated or headed a number of programs and organizations devoted to fostering science in education, particularly to providing support for schoolgirls interested in science, mathematics, or technology. She also wrote or collaborated on several children's books about space exploration and her personal experiences as an astronaut. Ride died in La Jolla, California, on July 23, 2012. In 2013 she was posthumously awarded the Presidential Medal of Freedom.

EMILY WARREN ROEBLING

(b. 1843—d. 1903)

The wife of Washington Roebling, the engineer in charge of building the Brooklyn Bridge, Emily Roebling distinguished herself by managing the construction after poor health confined her husband to bed for the last ten years of the project. She acted as secretary, messenger, and go-between for Washington Roebling and the engineers, contractors, and city officials involved in the project. She won the deep respect of the project engineers for her thorough understanding of engineering as well as for her grace and diplomacy in dealing with disagreements among various parties. Two plaques on the bridge commemorate her contribution to its construction.

In the years following the bridge's completion, Emily Roebling earned a law degree, becoming one of the first female lawyers in the state of New York. She traveled extensively, published *The Journal of the Reverend Silas Constant* (1903), and was active in the women's patriotic group Daughters of the American Revolution. In 1983, Citicorp and the National Women's Hall of Fame established the Emily award to honor women's achievements in business, science, and technology.

FLORENCE RENA SABIN

(b. 1871—d. 1953)

American anatomist and investigator of the lymphatic system Florence Rena Sabin was considered to be one of the leading women scientists of the United States.

Sabin was educated in Denver, Colorado, and in Vermont and graduated from Smith College in Massachusetts, in 1893. After teaching in Denver and at Smith to earn tuition money, she entered the Johns Hopkins University Medical School in Baltimore, Maryland, in 1896.

While a student she demonstrated a particular gift for laboratory work; her model of the brain stem of a newborn infant was widely reproduced for use as a teaching model in medical schools. After graduation in 1900 she interned at Johns Hopkins Hospital for a year and then returned to the medical school to conduct research under a fellowship awarded by the Baltimore Association for the Advancement of University Education of Women. In 1901 she published An Atlas of the Medulla and Midbrain, which became a popular medical text. In 1902, when Johns Hopkins finally abandoned its policy of not appointing women to its medical faculty, Sabin was named an assistant in anatomy, and she became in 1917 the school's first female full professor.

For a number of years Sabin's research centerd on the lymphatic system, and her demonstration that lymphatic vessels develop from a special layer of cells in certain fetal veins, rather than, as prevailing theory held, from intercellular spaces, established her as a researcher of the first rank. She then turned to the study of blood, blood vessels, and blood cells and made numerous discoveries regarding their origin and development. In 1924 she was elected president of the American Association of Anatomists, and in 1925 she was elected to the National Academy of Sciences; in both cases she was the first woman to be so honoured.

Also in 1925 she accepted an invitation to join the Rockefeller Institute for Medical Research (now Rockefeller University), where she was also the first woman member. There she conducted research on tuberculosis, particularly the role of monocytes in forming tubercles. In 1934 she published a biography of her early mentor at Johns Hopkins, *Franklin Paine Mall: The Story of a Mind.*

Sabin retired from the Rockefeller Institute in 1938 and moved to Denver, where in 1944 she was named by the governor to a planning committee on postwar public health problems. She drew up a plan and lobbied successfully for a complete reorganization of the state health department. In 1948 she was appointed head of the Denver health department and served in that post until resigning in 1953. She died a short time later that year, and the state of Colorado subsequently chose her as one of its two representatives in Statuary Hall of the U.S. Capitol.

SVETLANA YEVGENYEVNA SAVITSKAYA

(b. 1948)

Soviet cosmonaut Svetlana Yevgenyevna Savitskaya is the first woman to walk in space.

The daughter of World War II fighter ace Yevgeny Savitsky, Savitskaya showed an aptitude for aviation at an early age. By her 22nd birthday, she had recorded over 400 parachute jumps and had claimed the top spot at the World Aerobatic Championships. She earned an engineering degree from Moscow Aviation Institute in 1972 and was accepted as a test pilot candidate. She ultimately qualified to fly more than 20 different types of aircraft, earning a number of women's speed and altitude records in the process.

In 1980 Savitskaya was selected to join the Soviet space program, and she began training

Svetlana Yevgenyevna Savitskaya

for work with Soyuz and Salyut spacecraft. On Aug. 19, 1982, as part of the Soyuz T-7 mission to the Salyut 7 space station, she became the second woman to enter outer space. On her second trip to Salyut 7, she became the first woman to perform a space walk when, on July 25, 1984, she participated in welding experiments on the outer hull of the space station.

Savitskaya returned to Earth and took an executive position at the aerospace design bureau Energia. She transitioned into politics, and in 1989 she was elected to the Duma as a member of the Communist Party. She remained active in the Duma throughout the reforms of the 1990s, and by 2003 she had risen to the fourth highest position in the Communist Party's ranks. She served as the deputy chairperson for the Duma's defense committee and won reelection to her seat in December 2007.

ELLEN CHURCHILL SEMPLE
(b. 1863—d. 1932)

Ellen Churchill Semple was an American geographer known for promoting the view that the physical environment determines human history and culture, an idea that provoked much controversy until superseded by later antideterministic approaches.

Semple earned B.A. (1882) and M.A. (1891) degrees from Vassar College in Poughkeepsie, New York, and studied at the University of Leipzig with the German anthropogeographer Friedrich Ratzel. Although not allowed to matriculate at Leipzig, she attended Ratzel's lectures—sitting apart from the male students—and was permanently influenced by his methods and ideas.

Semple's subsequent career alternated periods of writing with periods of teaching at a number of institutions, including the University of Oxford, the University of Chicago, Columbia University, the University of Colorado, Wellesley College, and Clark University. She was professor of anthropogeography at Clark from 1923 until 1932. In 1921 she was elected president of the Association of American Geographers, the first woman to hold that office. Her scholarly works include *American History and Its Geographic Conditions* (1903), which was adopted as a textbook by several colleges, *Influences of Geographic Environment* (1911), and *The Geography of the Mediterranean Region* (1931).

HELEN SHARMAN

(b. 1963)

Helen Sharman is a British chemist and astronaut, the first British citizen to go into space.

Sharman received a bachelor's degree in chemistry from the University of Sheffield in 1984. After receiving a doctorate from Birbeck College, London, she worked first as an engineer in London and then as a chemist for Mars Confectionery Ltd.

In November 1989 she responded to a radio advertisement for astronauts and was selected from more than 13,000 applicants to be part of Project Juno, a commercial British cosmonaut mission. She underwent 18 months of rigorous training at the Yury Gagarin Cosmonaut Training Centre at Star City, Russia. The project was nearly called off because the Juno consortium could not raise the required funding. The mission was able to proceed with Soviet money; however, the British experiments were limited owing to budgetary concerns.

Sharman finally launched into space on May 18, 1991, as a research cosmonaut on board Soyuz TM-12 with two Soviet cosmonauts, commander Anatoly Artsebarsky and flight engineer Sergey Krikalyov. Soyuz TM-12 docked with the space station Mir on May 20. The mission lasted nearly eight days, during which time Sharman conducted medical and agricultural tests. She also communicated with British schoolchildren on the radio. Sharman returned to Earth aboard Soyuz TM-11 on May 26.

Sharman was on the short list of candidates when the European Space Agency selected astronauts in 1992 and 1998. However, she was not selected in the final astronaut groups. She was made an Officer of the Order of the British Empire in 1992.

MARY SOMERVILLE

(b. 1780—d. 1872)

M ary Somerville was a British science writer whose influential works synthesized many different scientific disciplines.

As a child, Fairfax had a minimal education. She was taught to read (but not write) by her mother. When she was 10 years old, she attended a boarding school for girls for one year in Musselburgh, Scot. Upon her return home, she began to educate herself from the family library. She was encouraged only by her uncle, Thomas Somerville, who helped her with Latin.

In 1804 Fairfax married a cousin, Samuel Greig, who was a captain in the Russian navy and the Russian consul in London. She continued to study mathematics, but, as she later wrote, "Although my husband did not prevent me from studying, I met with no sympathy whatever from him, as he had a very low opinion of the capacity of my sex." After Samuel's death in 1807, she had the freedom to dedicate herself to her mathematical studies. She was married again in 1812, to another cousin, William Somerville, who took pride in his wife's educational accomplishments. She began to study botany and geology. In 1816 the Somervilles moved to London, where they became friends with such eminent scientists as astronomers Sir William Herschel and Caroline Herschel, metallurgist William Hyde Wollaston, physicist Thomas Young, and mathematician Charles Babbage, who showed the Somervilles the mechanical calculators he was making. On a trip to Europe in 1817, Somerville met French physicist François Arago and French mathematician Pierre-Simon Laplace. She published her first scientific paper, *On the Magnetizing Power of the More Refrangible Solar Rays*, in 1826.

In 1827 Somerville was asked by the lawyer Henry Brougham to prepare for the Society for the Diffusion of Useful Knowledge—which intended to make good books available at low prices to the working class—a condensed version of Laplace's five-volume work *Traité de mécanique céleste* (*Celestial Mechanics*, 1798—1827), which offered a complete mechanical interpretation of the solar system. After four years

Somerville finished, but Brougham deemed the work too long. However, astronomer Sir John Herschel considered the book excellent and recommended *Mechanism of the Heavens* (1831) to another publisher. *Mechanism of the Heavens*'s introduction, in which Somerville summarized the current state of astronomical knowledge for the general reader, was published separately in 1832 as *Preliminary Dissertation to the Mechanism of the Heavens*. *Mechanism of the Heavens* was acclaimed by British mathematicians and astronomers. The Royal Society commissioned a marble bust of Somerville from sculptor Francis Chantrey. Somerville and Caroline Herschel were made the first women honorary members of the Royal Astronomical Society.

Somerville's next book, *The Connection of the Physical Sciences* (1834), was even more ambitious in summarizing astronomy, physics, geography, and meteorology. She wrote nine subsequent editions over the rest of her life to update it. In the third edition, published in 1836, she wrote that difficulties in calculating the position of Uranus may point to the existence of an undiscovered planet. This hint inspired British astronomer John Couch Adams to begin the calculations that ultimately led to the discovery of Neptune. In 1835, on the recommendation of Prime Minister Sir Robert Peel, Somerville received a pension of £200 per year (later £300) from the Civil List. The Somerville family went to Italy in 1838 because of her husband's ill health, and she spent the rest of her life there.

Somerville's next book, *Physical Geography* (2 vol., 1848), was the first textbook on the subject in English and her most popular work. *Physical Geography* was influential in that "political and arbitrary divisions are disregarded" and "man himself is viewed but as a fellow-inhabitant of the globe with other created things, yet influencing them to a certain extent by his actions, and influenced in return." While writing it, she was discouraged by the appearance of the first volume of German naturalist Alexander von Humboldt's *Kosmos* (1845), which covered similar subject matter. However, Sir John Herschel encouraged her to publish her book. Six editions of *Physical Geography* were published in her lifetime. In 1869 Somerville received the Patron's Medal of the Royal Geographical Society for *Physical Geography*. Her final book, *On Molecular and Microscopic Science* (2 vol., 1869), was not as well received as her previous works. Her autobiography, *Personal Recollections, from Early Life to Old Age* (1873), was edited by her daughter Martha and published posthumously.

NETTIE MARIA STEVENS

(b. 1861—d. 1912)

American biologist and geneticist Nettie Maria Stevens was one of the first scientists to find that sex is determined by a particular configuration of chromosomes.

Stevens's early life is somewhat obscure, although it is known that she taught school and attended the State Normal School (now Westfield State College) in Westfield, Massachusetts, in 1881—83. In 1896 she entered Stanford University, earning a B.A. in 1899 and an M.A. in 1900. She began doctoral studies in biology at Bryn Mawr College, which included a year of study (1901—02) at the Zoological Station in Naples, Italy, and at the Zoological Institute of the University of Würzburg, Germany. She received a Ph.D. from Bryn Mawr in 1903 and remained at the college as a research fellow in biology for a year, as reader in experimental morphology for another year, and as associate in experimental morphology from 1905 until her death.

Stevens's earliest field of research was the morphology and taxonomy of the ciliate protozoa; her first published paper, in 1901, had dealt with such a protozoan. She soon turned to cytology and the regenerative process. One of her major papers in that field was written in 1904 with zoologist and geneticist Thomas Hunt Morgan, who in 1933 would win the Nobel Prize for his work. Her investigations into regeneration led her to a study of differentiation in embryos and then to a study of chromosomes. In 1905, after experiments with the yellow mealworm (Tenebrio molitor), she published a paper in which she announced her finding that a particular combination of the chromosomes known as X and Y was responsible for the determination of the sex of an individual.

This discovery, also announced independently that year by Edmund Beecher Wilson of Columbia University, not only ended the long-standing debate over whether sex was a matter of heredity or embryonic environmental influence but also was the first firm link between a heritable characteristic and a particular chromosome. Stevens continued her research on the chromosome makeup of various insects, discovering supernumerary chromosomes in certain insects and the paired state of chromosomes in flies and mosquitoes.

KATHRYN SULLIVAN

(b. 1951)

American oceanographer and astronaut Kathryn Sullivan is the first American woman to walk in space.

Sullivan received a bachelor's degree in Earth sciences from the University of California, Santa Cruz, in 1973 and a doctorate in geology from Dalhousie University in Halifax, N.S., Can., in 1978. While at

Kathryn Sullivan

Dalhousie she participated in several oceanographic expeditions that studied the floors of the Atlantic and Pacific oceans.

In 1978 Sullivan was selected as an astronaut by the U.S. National Aeronautics and Space Administration (NASA). Her first spaceflight was aboard the space shuttle *Challenger* on the STS-41G mission (Oct. 5—13, 1984). Sullivan and mission specialist David Leetsma performed a 3.5-hour space walk in which they operated a system designed to show that satellites could be refueled in orbit.

Sullivan flew on two more spaceflights. On STS-31 (April 24—29, 1990), the space shuttle *Discovery* deployed the Hubble Space Telescope. On STS-45 (March 24—April 2, 1992), Sullivan was the payload commander of the Atmospheric Laboratory for Applications and Science, a laboratory on a pallet housed in the space shuttle *Atlantis*'s cargo bay that contained 12 experiments studying Earth's atmosphere.

Sullivan left NASA in 1993 and became chief scientist at the National Oceanic and Atmospheric Administration (NOAA). In 1996 she was named president and chief executive officer of the Center of Science and Industry, a science museum in Columbus, Ohio. In 2006 Sullivan became the director of the Battelle Center for Mathematics and Science Education Policy at Ohio State University in Columbus. In 2011, Pres. Barack Obama appointed her assistant secretary of commerce for environmental observation and prediction and deputy administrator of NOAA.

HELEN BROOKE TAUSSIG

(b. 1898—d. 1986)

Helen Brooke Taussig was an American physician recognized as the founder of pediatric cardiology, best known for her contributions to the development of the first successful treatment of "blue baby" syndrome.

Helen Taussig was born into a distinguished family as the daughter of Frank and Edith Guild Taussig. Her father was a prominent economics professor at Harvard University, and her mother was one of the first women to attend Radcliffe College (today known as the Radcliffe Institute for Advanced Study), an extension of Harvard that provided instruction for women. Although Taussig enjoyed a privileged upbringing, adversity cultivated in her a determination that later defined her character. As a child, the dyslexic Taussig laboured to become proficient in reading and was tutored by her father, who recognized the potential of her logical mind. When Taussig was 11, her mother died of tuberculosis, an illness Helen would later contract as well. However, these obstacles did not discourage Taussig from obtaining a university education. She enrolled at Radcliffe College in 1917, transferring to the University of California, Berkeley, in 1919, where she earned an A.B. in 1921. Taussig aspired to study medicine at Harvard but was denied admission because the university did not accept women into its academic degree program. Instead, she attended the Boston University School of Medicine from 1922 to 1924 and graduated from the Johns Hopkins University School of Medicine in 1927.

Two individuals had a far-reaching impact on Taussig's career. First was Canadian pathologist Maude Abbott of McGill University in Montreal. Abbott was a strong-minded role model whose earlier studies of congenital heart disease created the foundation for Taussig's own research into heart disease. Then, while an intern at Johns Hopkins, Taussig's work attracted the attention of American pediatrician Edwards A. Park, the director and, later, the chief of pediatrics at Johns Hopkins. In 1930 Park elevated Taussig to director of Hopkins' Harriet Lane Clinic, a health care center for children, making her one of the first women in the country to hold such a prestigious position.

Taussig's career advanced, but her personal challenges mounted. In her 30s she grew deaf, and as a result she developed an innovative method to explore the beat of the human heart using her hands to compensate for her hearing loss. Relying on this method, Taussig noticed common beat patterns in the malformed hearts of infant patients who outwardly displayed a cyanotic hue and hence were known as "blue babies." She traced the root of the problem to a lack of oxygenated blood circulating from the lungs to the heart. Taussig reasoned that the creation of an arterial patent ductus, or shunt, would alleviate the problem, and she championed the cause before American surgeon Alfred Blalock,

Hopkins' chief of the department of surgery. Together they developed the Blalock-Taussig shunt, an artery-like tube designed to deliver oxygen-rich blood from the lungs to the heart. On November 29, 1944, Eileen Saxton, an infant affected by tetralogy of Fallot, a congenital heart disorder that gives rise to blue baby syndrome and that was previously considered untreatable, became the first patient to survive a successfully implanted Blalock-Taussig shunt. The miracle surgery was touted in the American magazines *Time* and *Life*, as well as in newspapers around the world. Later, American laboratory technician Vivien Thomas was also recognized for his contributions to the surgery.

Taussig was a prolific writer, publishing an astounding number of medical papers. In 1947 she wrote *Congenital Malformations of the Heart*, which was revised in 1960. Throughout her lifetime she received world-wide honours. She was awarded the Medal of Freedom by U.S. President Lyndon B. Johnson in 1964, and in 1965 Taussig became the first woman president of the American Heart Association. In addition, Taussig testified before the U.S. Congress about the harmful effects of the drug thalidomide, which had produced deformed children in Europe.

Taussig's ideas and determination have had long-lasting impacts on cardiology. Physicians originally believed the early blue babies could possibly endure a 40-year life span. At the turn of the 21st century, some of these early patients continued to survive into their sixth decade.

VALENTINA TERESHKOVA

(b. 1937)

Valentina Tereshkova, a Soviet cosmonaut, is the first woman to travel in space. Her spacecraft, *Vostok 6*, was launched on June 16, 1963. It completed 48 orbits of Earth in 71 hours before landing safely. In space at the same time was fellow cosmonaut Valeri F. Bykovsky, who had been launched two days earlier in *Vostok 5*. His craft also landed on June 19.

Tereshkova was born on March 6, 1937, in Maslennikovo, Russian S.F.S.R., near the larger city of Yaroslavl. Because her father was killed early in World War II, her early life was difficult. She did not begin schooling until age 10, and by age 17 she was an apprentice at the Yaroslavl tire factory. She became an ardent Communist, joined the Komsomol (Communist Youth League), and took up parachuting as a hobby. Her work in the Komsomol and her devotion and expertise in parachute jumping helped her win a chance at being a cosmonaut. In 1961 she became a member of the Communist Party.

That same year Yuri Gagarin had become the first man to orbit Earth. Inspired by his feat, she applied to become a cosmonaut. In spite of the fact that she had no training as a pilot, she was accepted for the Soviet space program in 1962.

After her flight she left the space program and married cosmonaut Andriyan G. Nikolayev. She also became an active and powerful member of the Supreme Soviet. In 1968 Tereshkova was chosen to head the Soviet Women's Committee. From 1974 she served as a member of the Supreme Soviet Presidium. She was awarded the Order of Lenin twice.

MARY WATSON WHITNEY

(b. 1847—d. 1921)

American astronomer Mary Watson Whitney built Vassar College's research program in astronomy into one of the nation's finest.

Whitney graduated from public high school in 1863 and entered Vassar College, Poughkeepsie, New York, with advanced standing in 1865. She immediately came under the influence of the astronomer Maria Mitchell. After graduating in 1868 Whitney returned to Waltham for a time to care for her widowed mother, then taught school in Auburndale, Massachusetts. In 1869 she traveled to Burlington, Iowa, to observe a solar eclipse with her own three-inch Alvan Clark telescope. From 1869 to 1870 she attended, on invitation, Benjamin Peirce's class in quaternions at Harvard and his private class in celestial mechanics. In 1872 Vassar granted her a master's degree. She then studied mathematics and celestial mechanics at the University of Zürich, Switzerland (1873—76).

Whitney taught at Waltham High School (1876–81) before returning to Vassar as Maria Mitchell's assistant. In 1888 she succeeded Mitchell as professor of astronomy and director of the college observatory. Whitney proved to be a popular and effective teacher. Her determination to demonstrate the capacity of women to work in the sciences on equal terms with men led to her development of an ambitious program of research at Vassar, concentrating in particular on double stars, variable stars, asteroids, comets, and the precise measurement of photographic plates. With such training, her students were able to find professional positions in observatories across the country. In 1899 Whitney was a founding member of the American Astronomical Society. She retired from Vassar for health reasons in 1910.

PEGGY WHITSON

(b. 1960)

American biochemist and astronaut Peggy Whitson was the first female commander of the International Space Station (ISS). She set a record among American astronauts and among women for spending the most time in space.

Peggy A. Whitson was born on Feb. 9, 1960, in Mount Ayr, Iowa. She received a B.S. in biology and chemistry from Iowa Wesleyan College in Mount Pleasant, Iowa, in 1981 and a doctorate in biochemistry from Rice University in Houston in 1985. In 1986 she moved to the National Aeronautics and Space Administration's (NASA's) Johnson Space Center (JSC) in Houston as a research associate and later worked as the supervisor for the Biochemistry Research Group at KRUG International, a NASA medical sciences contractor at the JSC. Whitson had a long and varied career at NASA before her selection as an astronaut candidate. Among other positions, she worked in the Biomedical Operations and Research branch at the JSC from 1989 to 1993 and was the deputy division chief of the Medical Sciences Division at the JSC from 1993 to 1996. She also participated in joint efforts between American and Soviet (later Russian) scientists.

Whitson began her astronaut training in August 1996. After completing two years of training, she worked in various technical positions at the Operations Planning branch of NASA's Astronaut Office. She flew into space for the first time on June 5, 2002, as a flight engineer on Expedition 5 to the ISS, aboard the space shuttle *Endeavour* on mission STS-111. On board the ISS, she conducted more than 20 experiments in microgravity and human life sciences and also operated and installed commercial payloads and hardware systems. She was designated as the first NASA ISS science officer and also performed a space walk to install shielding on a service module and to deploy a science payload. After nearly 185 days in space, she returned to Earth aboard STS-113, landing on December 7.

Peggy Whitson (*right*) with astronaut Pam Melroy

Whitson traveled into space for a second time on Oct. 10, 2007 — aboard Soyuz TMA-11 with Yury Malenchenko of Russia and Sheikh Muszaphar Shukor of Malaysia — as the commander of the Expedition 16 mission. The first female commander of the ISS, Whitson supervised and directed a significant expansion of the living and working space on the ISS, including the installation of components made by European, Japanese, and Canadian space agencies. During the six-month mission she also performed five space walks to carry out maintenance and assembly tasks. After spending nearly 192 days in space, Whitson returned to Earth aboard Soyuz TMA-11 on April 19, 2008. The crew of Soyuz TMA-11 had a difficult and dangerous ride back to Earth; the Soyuz's equipment module failed to separate properly from the reentry module, and so the craft followed an unusually steep descent trajectory. The crew made an extremely hard landing, which missed the target by 470 km (300 miles). Whitson suffered no permanent injuries.

Whitson spent nearly 377 days in space during her two long-duration tours of duty to the ISS, which made her NASA's most experienced astronaut. Her total of six career space walks and their combined duration of 39 hours 46 minutes were records for a female astronaut. In 2009 she became chief of the Astronaut Office, which oversees all NASA astronaut activities, including crew selection and training.

SUNITA WILLIAMS

(b. 1965)

American astronaut Sunita Williams holds the record for most time spent on space walks by a woman.

In 1983 Williams entered the U.S. Naval Academy at Annapolis, Maryland. She was made an ensign in 1987 and reported for aviator training at the Naval Aviation Training Command. In July 1989 she began combat helicopter training. She flew in helicopter support squadrons during the preparations for the Persian Gulf War and the establishment of no-fly zones over Kurdish areas of Iraq, as well as in relief missions during Hurricane Andrew in 1992 in Miami.

In 1993 she became a naval test pilot, and she later became a test pilot instructor, flying more than 30 different aircraft and logging more than 2,770 flight hours. When selected for the astronaut program, she was stationed aboard the USS Saipan.

Williams completed an M.S. in engineering management from the Florida Institute of Technology in Melbourne in 1995, and she entered astronaut training in 1998. She traveled to Moscow, where she received training in robotics and other International Space Station (ISS) operational technologies while working with the Russian Federal Space Agency and with crews preparing for expeditions to the ISS.

On December 9, 2006, Williams flew aboard the space shuttle *Discovery* on the STS-116 mission to the ISS, where she was a flight engineer for Expeditions 14 and 15. During her stay at the space station, she made four space walks, totaling more than 29 hours outside the spacecraft, and spent a total of more than 195 days in space, both of which were records for women in space. (She held the latter record until 2015, when Italian astronaut Samantha Cristoforetti spent more than 199 days in space.) She also participated in the Boston Marathon by running 42.2 km (26.2 miles) on the station's treadmill. She was the second American astronaut of Indian heritage to go into space, after Kalpana Chawla, who died in the *Columbia* disaster. Williams landed at Edwards Air Force Base in California with the crew of STS-117 on June 22, 2007.

Williams flew to the ISS again on July 15, 2012, as part of the crew of Soyuz TMA-05M. She was a flight engineer on Expedition 32, and on September 16 she became commander of Expedition 33. She made three more space walks, totaling more than 21 hours, retaining her space walk record with a total time outside the ISS between her two flights of more than 50 hours. She also completed a triathlon in orbit by using a treadmill, a stationary bicycle, and a weightlifting machine to simulate the swimming portion of the race. Williams returned to Earth on November 11 after nearly 127 days in space. Her two space-flights combined lasted more than 321 days, making her second, after

Sunita Williams

American astronaut Peggy Whitson, for the most time spent in space by a woman.

In 2015 Williams was selected as one of four astronauts to make the first test flights in NASA's Commercial Crew program, in which two new private crewed spacecraft, SpaceX's Dragon and Boeing's CST-100, would take astronauts and supplies to the ISS. Flights were scheduled to begin in 2017.

CHIEN-SHIUNG WU

(b. 1912—d. 1997)

The Chinese-born physicist Chien-shiung Wu provided the first experimental proof that the principle of parity conservation does not hold in weak subatomic interactions.

Wu was born on May 31, 1912, in Liuho, Jiangsu Province. She went to the United States in 1936 to study at the University of California in Berkeley. After receiving her doctorate in 1940, she taught at Smith College, in Northampton, Mass., and at Princeton University, in Princeton, N.J. In 1944 she worked on radiation detection in the Division of War Research at Columbia University, in New York City, and became professor of physics in 1957.

After the early 1930s conservation of parity, or symmetry, became a fundamental theory in quantum mechanics. In 1956 the theoretical physicists Tsung-Dao Lee and Chen Ning Yang proposed that parity is not conserved for one of the three basic nuclear interactions—weak interactions, which govern radioactive decay. In 1957 Wu proved them right by showing that the beta particles given off by cobalt-60 atoms have a preferred direction. Wu and others confirmed the conservation of vector current in nuclear beta decay in 1963. She also studied the structure of hemoglobin. Wu received the National Medal of Science in 1975 and served as president of the American Physical Society in 1975. She died in New York City on Feb. 16, 1997.

ROSALYN SUSSMAN YALOW

(b. 1921—d. 2011)

A merican medical physicist Rosalyn Sussman Yalow was a joint recipient of the 1977 Nobel Prize for Physiology or Medicine. She was awarded the prize for her development of radioimmunoassay (RIA), a technique for measuring levels of insulin (a hormone that regulates the level of sugar, or glucose, in the blood) and other substances in the body. The two other award recipients in 1977 were Andrew V. Schally and Roger Guillemin.

Rosalyn Sussman Yalow was born on July 19, 1921, in New York, New York. She graduated from Hunter College of the City University of New York in 1941 and four years later received a doctorate in physics from the University of Illinois. From 1946 to 1950 Yalow lectured on physics at Hunter College, and in 1947 she became a consultant in nuclear physics to the Bronx Veterans Administration Medical Center (now James J. Peters VA Medical Center). There, from 1950 to 1970, she was physicist and assistant chief of the radioisotope service. In 1970 she was appointed chief of the laboratory.

With a colleague, the American physician Solomon A. Berson, Yalow began using radioactive isotopes to examine and diagnose various disease conditions. Yalow and Berson's investigations into type II diabetes led to their development of RIA.

In the 1950s it was known that individuals with diabetes who were treated with injections of animal insulin developed resistance to that hormone. This resistance meant that the individuals required greater amounts of insulin to offset the effects of the disease. However, researchers did not know why. Yalow and Berson theorized that the foreign insulin stimulated the production of antibodies (protective proteins produced by the immune system that rid the body of antigens, or foreign substances). These antibodies became bound to the insulin and prevented the hormone from entering cells and carrying out its function of metabolizing glucose.

In order to prove their hypothesis, Yalow and Berson combined techniques from immunology and radioisotope tracing to measure minute amounts of these antibodies, thus creating RIA. It was soon apparent that the RIA method could be used to measure hundreds of other biologically active substances, such as viruses, drugs, and other proteins.

Yalow remained in New York for the rest of her career, where she became a distinguished professor at large at two different medical schools. In 1976 she was the first female recipient of the Albert Lasker Basic Medical Research Award, and in 1988 she was awarded the National Medal of Science. Yalow died on May 30, 2011, in New York City.

YI SOYEON

(b. 1978)

South Korean scientist and astronaut Yi Soyeon is the first South Korean citizen in space.

She earned bachelor's and master's degrees in mechanical engineering at the Korea Advanced Institute of Science and Technology (KAIST) in Taejŏn in 2001 and 2002, respectively. In 2006 she was working toward a doctorate in biological science at KAIST when she was one of two finalists selected from 36,000 applicants to train in Russia for a flight to the International Space Station (ISS). South Korea paid Russia $20 million to allow a South Korean cosmonaut to accompany the Russian spaceflight. Yi was trained as a backup to computer engineer Ko San. The Russian Federal Space Agency, however, barred Ko from the mission for violations of training protocol after he removed reading materials from a training center and mailed classified documents to South Korea.

On April 8, 2008, Yi blasted off from the Baikonur Cosmodrome in Kazakhstan as a payload specialist alongside two Russian cosmonauts, commander Sergey Volkov and flight engineer Oleg Kononenko. Their Soyuz TMA-12 craft docked with the ISS, where Yi spent nine days carrying out experiments and medical tests. She returned on April 19 with two returning space station crew members, American commander Peggy Whitson and Russian flight engineer Yury Malenchenko, aboard Soyuz TMA-11. Although the mission was a success, the Soyuz's equipment

Yi Soyeon

module failed to separate properly from the reentry module, and so the craft followed an unusually steep trajectory to Earth and made a rough landing in the Kazakhstan steppes, during which Yi sustained back injuries that later required her hospitalization.

ADA YONATH

(b. 1939)

Israeli protein crystallographer Ada Yonath was awarded the 2009 Nobel Prize for Chemistry, along with Indian-born American physicist and molecular biologist Venkatraman Ramakrishnan and American biophysicist and biochemist Thomas Steitz, for her research into the atomic structure and function of cellular particles called ribosomes. (Ribosomes are tiny particles made up of RNA and proteins that specialize in protein synthesis and are found free or bound to the endoplasmic reticulum within cells.)

Yonath received a bachelor's degree in chemistry in 1962 and a master's degree in biochemistry in 1964 from Hebrew University in Jerusalem. She then attended the Weizmann Institute of Science in Israel as a graduate student, studying X-ray crystallography and receiving a Ph.D. in 1968. After a brief stint as a postdoctoral researcher at Carnegie Mellon University in Pittsburgh, Pa., Yonath joined the department of chemistry at the Massachusetts Institute of Technology (MIT) as a postdoctoral fellow. There she began investigating the structure of ribosomes using X-ray crystallography and pioneered the development of new approaches to the study of structural characteristics of large, complex molecules.

From 1970 to 1974 Yonath worked as a scientist in the department of chemistry at the Weizmann Institute. She later became senior scientist (1974–83), associate professor (1984–88), and director of the Mazer Center for Structural Biology (1988–2004). She also was director of the Kimmelman Center for Biomolecular Structure and Assembly at the Weizmann Institute (1989–) and served as head of the Max Planck Research Unit for Ribosomal Structure in Germany (1986–2004). In

Ada Yonath

1980 Yonath became the first person to determine the three-dimensional atomic arrangement of a large ribosomal subunit (ribosomes consist of two distinct subunits, one large and one small). She conducted these early studies using ribosomes from the bacterium Bacillus stearothermophilus. Her subsequent research revealed the complex architecture of ribosomes, and she identified structures resembling tunnels, through which newly synthesized polypeptide chains were passed during protein synthesis.

Yonath's other achievements include the development of a technique known as cryocrystallography, in which protein crystals are rapidly cooled, thereby overcoming the limitation of radiation damage to protein crystals that is associated with traditional X-ray crystallography techniques. She also successfully determined the atomic structure of the small ribosomal subunit of Thermus thermophilus (a bacterium widely used in genetics research), obtaining a structural resolution of 3.3 angstroms (Å; 1 Å is equivalent to 10^{-10} meter, or 0.1 nanometer). Her later research was concerned with determining the atomic structures of antibiotics, focusing especially on how the atomic structures of these agents influence their activities and interactions with cellular machinery.

Yonath was elected a member of the Israel Academy of Sciences and Humanities in 2000 and the U.S. National Academy of Sciences in 2003. In addition to the 2009 Nobel Prize, she received numerous other honours and awards throughout her career, including the Louisa Gross Horwitz Prize for Biology or Biochemistry in 2005, the Paul Ehrlich and Ludwig Darmstaedter Prize in 2007, and the Albert Einstein World Award of Science in 2008.

GLOSSARY

ABOLITION The act of officially ending or stopping something; the act of abolishing something, specifically the act of abolishing slavery.

ACCREDITED To say that something is good enough to be given official approval.

ANESTHESIOLOGIST A doctor who specializes in anesthesia and anesthetics.

ANTHROPOLOGY The study of human races, origins, societies, and cultures.

BIOCHEMISTRY The chemistry of living things.

BIOPHYSICS A branch of science concerned with the application of physical principles and methods to biological problems.

BOTANY A branch of science that deals with plant life.

CHROMOSOME The part of a cell that contains the genes that control how an animal or plant grows and what it becomes.

COMMUNICABLE Able to be passed to another person.

COMPUTER SCIENCE The study of computers and their uses.

CONVALESCE To become healthy and strong again slowly over time after illness, weakness, or injury.

DIFFERENTIAL CALCULUS A branch of mathematics concerned chiefly with the study of the rate of change of functions with respect to their variables especially through the use of derivatives and differentials.

ENTOMOLOGY A branch of science that deals with the study of insects.

EVOLUTION A theory that the differences between modern plants and animals are because of changes that happened by a natural process over a very long time.

GENETICS The scientific study of how genes control the characteristics of plants and animals.

HYDRODYNAMICS A branch of physics that deals with the motion of fluids and the forces acting on solid bodies immersed in fluids and in motion relative to them.

MICROBIOLOGY A science that studies extremely small forms of life (such as bacteria and viruses).

NATURALIST A person who studies plants and animals as they live in nature.

PALEONTOLOGY The science that deals with the fossils of animals and plants that lived very long ago especially in the time of dinosaurs.

PANDEMIC Occurring over a wide geographic area and affecting an exceptionally high proportion of the population.

PRODIGY A young person who is unusually talented in some way.

SUPERCOMPUTER A large and very fast computer.

TUBERCULOSIS A serious disease that mainly affects the lungs.

ZOOLOGY The branch of science that involves the study of animals and animal behavior.

INDEX